The Drinking and Eating Guide to the BVI

by

Julian Putley

Published by
Virgin Island Books
P.O. Box 8309 • Cruz Bay, St. John
US Virgin Islands 00831
e-mail: putley@surfbvi.com

Illustrations by Hannah Welch

The Drinking and Eating Guide to the BVI

The Drinking and Eating Guide to the BVI now enters its fourth edition. Every year this little guide book finds more and more fans and is proof that sailing from Caribbean bar to bar, seafood restaurant to bbq joint is on everyone's list of essential fun activities.

The D&E Guide to the BVI is about FUN. In fact that's what a holiday in the BVI is all about. It's just so dazzlingly beautiful with great beach bars, nightspots and party venues around every corner. So while you're relaxing under the tropical sun, sailing away on a beautiful yacht to palm lined powdery beaches or waiting to dive into warm azure waters just peruse this guide and let the good times roll – cos fun is on the menu. It is often quoted that if you can't have fun here, you can't have fun anywhere.

Nearly every evening of a Caribbean holiday will involve visiting a beach bar, club or nightspot where reggae, calypso, blues or steel pan music will be playing. This guide shows you the best places to go with FREE drinks, favorite food and drink recipes and special happenings.

The Caribbean has long been noted for its calypso songs; spontaneous topical commentary that usually concerns everyday life, family or political scandal in humorous ways, often with sexual nuance. World famous Foxy may well come up with a personalized rendition as you wonder into his beach bar.

The clever cartoons are by talented graphic artist Hannah Welch. The short stories and limericks are by Julian Putley and are sure to bring a smile to the face of even the most world weary

A Note on the Free Offers and Giveaways

In keeping with the fun nature of this book most bars are offering free drinks and giveaways. Sailors' Rest, Neptune's Treasure and Myett's are giving away a free bottle of wine per table with dinner. Nearly every bar is giving away a free specialty drink, tropical cocktail or rum smoothie.

In the back of the book are coupons. All you do is take the book with you to the bar and show them the coupon so that they can void it and supply you with their special offer. DO NOT cut out the coupons, as they will then be valueless. Then keep the book as a souvenir of your pub crawl around the BVI.

Jost Van Dyke

NOT TO BE USED FOR NAVIGATION

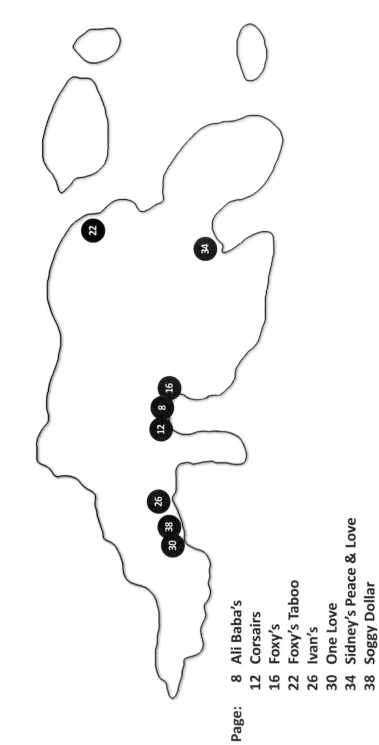

Tortola

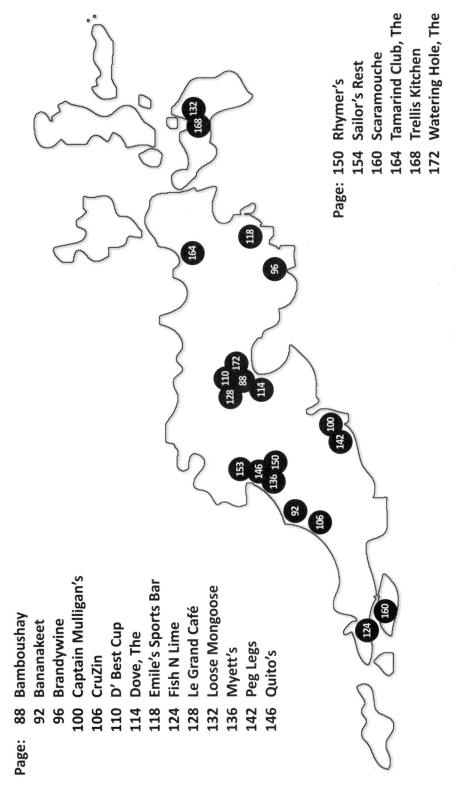

5

Virgin Gorda

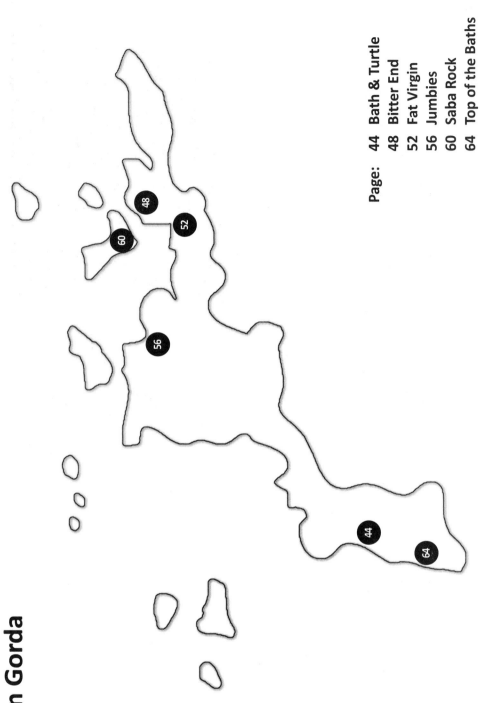

Anegada

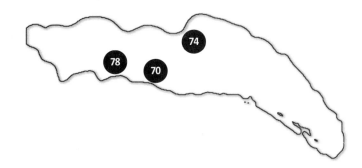

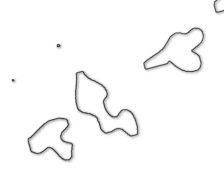

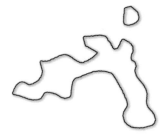

Norman Island

ALI BABA's
GREAT HARBOUR
JOST VAN DYKE

Ali Baba's

**Open 7 days. Breakfast, Lunch and Dinner
  (No Lunch on Sunday)
West Indian Fare with a Flare
Barbecue on Monday and Wednesday
Spectacular home crafted jewelry and souvenirs
Central Location on Great Harbor's Waterfront**

Tel: 495-9280 • VHF: Ch 16

*Free BBC
or Paralyser
(2 for 1)*

Ali Baba's is centrally located just off the beach in Jost van Dyke's Great Harbor. The airy ambiance and al fresco dining make this a perfect restaurant choice. There are delicious items on the menu like black bean soup, garlic butter shrimp and hot chicken wings. Other items include a boneless chicken roti, stewed conch, fresh fish and barbecued chicken.

Hammocks at the water's edge are ideal for lounging with one of Ali Baba's famous tropical cocktails.

A unique fact of Ali Baba's is his fine display of hand crafted jewelry and exotic souvenirs. The conch shell lamps are especially attractive mounted on a base of varnished mahogany.

Ali Baba's has a room to rent and they offer a free night if you stay a week. It's a great location and especially convenient for those big JVD party events.

| Cryptic Comment |

**Forgive your enemy,
but remember the ass-hole's name.**

Specialty Drinks

BBC

Ingredients: 1 shot amber rum
                1 shot Baileys
                Sliced banana, pineapple
                Coco Lopez

Method: Mix ingredients in a blender with ice, garnish with a cherry

Paralyser

Ingredients: 1 shot Vodka
                1 shot Kahlua
                Coco Lopez

Method: Stir ingredients together and pour over ice cubes

Specialty Dish

BBQ

Ali Baba's specialty is the twice weekly barbecue. On Monday barbecued pork is on the menu, sometimes a whole pig. The barbecues here are spiced with a local bbq creole sauce, whose recipe originated in Santo Domingo. On Wednesday the barbecued offerings include fresh fish, chicken and ribs and are accompanied by corn, peas and rice, pasta and a selection of tropical fruit.

Ali Baba's

Ali Baba's

Baba's is right on the beach
It's really within easy reach
Stroll in the water
Cos that's what you aught ta
Do in a place that's a 'peach'

Try stew conch, it's really the best
No, I'm not making a jest
Go on, please your wife
It'll help your sex life
She'll say the islands are blessed

Something special for you to own
Don't worry, you won't need a loan
It's a conch shell light
They're so 'out o' sight'
It'll light up your bedroom at home

Corsairs

**Great Food, Great Drinks,
Great Harbor (JVD)
Breakfast, Lunch and Dinner**

**Home of the 16oz Rib Eye and
'Monster Lobster'
Voted Best Pizzas in the Islands**

Tel: 495-9294 • VHF: Ch 16 • www.corsairsbvi.com
E mail: corsairsjvd@gmail.com

Corsairs is one of the most popular bar and eateries in Jost van Dyke. Hosts Vinny and Debbie will welcome you and describe their specials and large selection of pizzas, for which they are famous. Their location smack dab in the middle of Great Harbour, minutes from the main dock is very convenient. They can also do sushi platters given 24 hour notice. Other dishes which are popular include seared tuna with tango-mango rum sauce and surf and turf. Their special 'bone-in' rib eye is huge at 16 oz and will satisfy the most hungry sailor. Corsairs puts the naughty into nautical. You can tell it's a fun location: their motto is 'Sobriety is not our Priority.'

Cryptic Comment

**Fighting for Peace is
like Screwing for Virginity.**

Specialty Drink

Wench Juice

Ingredients: 1 glass, 1 shot of Corsairs rum

Method: Pour rum in glass and swallow

Specialty Dish

Fire Roasted Rib Eye

Ingredients: One 16oz bone-in rib eye steak.
                 Corsairs special rub

Method: This monster steak is rubbed with the special seasoning and fire
                 roasted to your exact specifications – rare to well done.
                 The dish is served with Corsairs famous fries and a medley of
                 fresh vegetables. Those with a very hearty appetite are invited
                 to pair this with a 'Monster Lobster' to make a surf and turf
                 to die for.

Cryptic Comment

**If you help someone
when they're in trouble, they will remember
you when they're in trouble again.**

Corsairs

Corsairs

T'was the home of the Buccaneers
In yesterday's bygone years
Now an American Biker
Has turned Jost van Dyker
And serves grub 'n very cold beers

It's still known as a pirate bar
People come from near and from far
To taste the food
That's ever so good
With fat bellies you can hear 'em, "Oh! Aaaarrrh!"

Cryptic Comment

The NASA robot landed on Mars recently. There seemed to be no sports channels, beer or porn, making it quite obvious that men are NOT from Mars.

Foxy's

World Famous Party Bar and Restaurant
"The place where friends are met
and memories made"

Free Giveaway
Born 'ere Beer

Tel: 495-9275 • VHF: Ch 16 • www.foxysbar.com

Foxy's is, without a doubt, the most famous beach bar in the Virgin Islands, if not the entire Caribbean. It started from small beginnings in 1968 with a lean-to affair next to the church in Great Harbour on Jost van Dyke's south side, erected temporarily to supply refreshments for an island fete. After that Foxy's moved to its present location behind the palms at the eastern end of the bay but for years it was only a simple palm frond shack. In those early days there were no bareboats but crews and guests of large yachts needed a good watering hole with cold beer and quality rum, and Foxy's was there. Often it was a help your-self arrangement and Foxy would sometimes call in between fishing trips and tell a story or two. His magnetic personality endeared him to everyone.

In 1974 two sailors were drinking rum at the bar and arguing the merits of their two boats and when the arguing got to loud gesticulating it was Foxy who suggested a race: the first wooden boat race was born. The music at the party that night was a local scratch band with Ruben Chinnery playing lead and today he is still one of the islands' most popular entertainers. And there you have it, the recipe for success: tropical shack, laid back style, rum drinks and cold beer, a happy, story-telling host and great music.

Today the ambiance is not much different to what it was in those early days. There's a popular restaurant, a gift shop and the bar is festooned with memen-tos from thousands of visitors and years of parties: their annual wooden boat race has just concluded and the winners of the various categories will have their names carved into the prestigious name boards.

Now mega parties are organized at Christmas and Old Year's Night and sometimes the new stadium out back is used for private parties. One recent one for a fiftieth birthday party hired The Beach Boys, who flew down with a large entourage for the one night show. Yep, Foxy's has come a long way.

But the magic of Foxy's is that the old-time flavor has been retained while hundreds of visitors are welcomed, watered, fed and entertained daily. Foxy, barefoot, baggy pants and knotty dreads poking out from under a baseball cap will play an impromptu calypso that will be about the most topical event. He'll laugh at you...and then he'll laugh at himself...and then he'll laugh with you. Wife Tessa, not far in the background, will be choreographing the day's business activities and everything seems to roll along with so little effort that visitors go away shaking their heads in wonder.

In the words of one of the locals "It jus' a Jost van Dyke ting."

Specialty Drink

Dread Fox

Ingredients: 1 shot Foxy's Firewater
1 shot Silver Fox Rum
Margarita Mix
Cranberry Juice

Method: Mix all the ingredients with a twist of fresh lime.
Pour over ice cubes and finish with freshly grated nutmeg

Specialty Dish

West Indian Buffet

"Every Friday and Saturday we fire up the Grillzebo to prepare a BBQ known around the world and our entertainment features the best in local bands. Our famous Caribbean BBQ boasts fresh salads, fruits, vegetables, BBQ Chicken, Ribs (like you've never had before), and Mahi-Mahi that melts in your mouth!"

Foxy's

Foxy's

Twas a party night in town
New Year's had come around
The bay was packed
Then the wind, it backed
And boats just ran aground

The moon aligned with Mars
It outshone all the stars
Then late that night
Skies filled with light
From rockets fired from bars

Twas ol' year's night at Foxy's
The bar was full of hotties
The band played on
Till the sun, it shone
New year was here
To me twas clear
Foxy's just has no copies

Cryptic Comment

Partners help each other undress before sex. However after sex, they always dress on their own.

Moral of the story: In life, no one helps you once you're screwed.

The recession is here and it looks like it may turn into a depression. Charlie has been racking his brains to think of fun, lucrative business opportunities to help out his fellow sailors. One thing that Charlie noticed recently is that many new boats are equipped with electric winches. It seems that the days of deck apes and tortuous winch grinding at every tack is on the way out. Now it's gonna be 'push button' sailing. Gone will be the need for sailing gloves to protect pampered hands. Charlie has just patented three new sailing accoutrements, the index finger protector, the middle finger protector and the big toe protector. They come in a multitude of colours and sizes, the larger size for larger buttons (obviously for bigger yachts). Charlie anticipates that the large red middle finger protector will be the best seller. It has the dual purpose of protecting the finger from wear and tear and also is quite conspicuous when giving the finger to competitors when you're about to leave them in your wake.

Just last week (end March) Charlie received his Christmas mail – just a few days after an E mail message from his old Mum in England who said, quite bluntly, 'You f...ing reprobate, you could at least send a thank you note.' Charlie's second business idea was born. He will be offering a postal service from Europe to the Caribbean by sail boat. He anticipates it will cut weeks off the traditional snail mail service and be more environmentally friendly. He'll sail over to Europe in late summer. Pick up mail in November in the UK, France, Spain, Portugal and Gibraltar (with a feeder service from the rest of Europe). Depart the Canaries late November and arrive in the Caribbean before Christmas. Emblazoned across his main sail will be the words, 'Express Mail.' All his sailing expenses will be written off and he'll cruise the coasts of some of the best wine growing and cheese producing regions in the world.

Charlie has just E mailed his Mum: 'Thanks Mum, I luv ya!'

The Season

In the Caribbean when October comes around people get ready for *The Season*. But what exactly does this ambiguous term really mean. Someone once told me that in New Hampshire they have four seasons: the wet season, the mud season, the fly season and the off season. Still want to visit? Really, of course, in the northern hemisphere north of the tropics, there are four seasons directed by the earth's revolution around the sun, winter, spring, summer and autumn (fall, to those challenged by the English language). In the tropics we typically have two seasons, the wet season and the dry season, but in recent decades the seasons refer more to visitor arrivals than to climate change. The high season is from Christmas to May, May to August is summer season, August to November is hurricane season and November to Christmas is ....well, shoulder season.

By December those in the tourist industry are usually anxiously awaiting the arrival of well heeled visitors from northern climes: empty pockets are in need. Conversely by August the stress and strain of continuous tourist arrivals along with the ubiquitous tedious and mundane questions make employees wish they had chosen an exciting career in accounting.

To those who find tourists unbearable there is a solution: it is to be found in the above mentioned fly season of states in New England. Apparently it is possible to become at least partially immune to the nasty stinging bites of the voracious insects. Some years ago a man wearing a wide-brimmed black hat attracted hundreds of the bothersome critters. By sweeping his hand across the top of his swarming head gear he caught and then, in a rage, ate the offending flies. Hey presto! He became instantly immune; he was never bitten again.

So next time bothersome tourists become insufferable eat a few of them. Word will soon spread and visitor arrivals will drop to a more manageable level. After all it worked for the Fiji group when Captain Bligh was chased by a canoe full of savage natives screaming, "Faster, faster, long pig for dinner tonight!" Although Bligh escaped, tourism, even today, comes only in fits and starts.

There is one caveat: To owners and managers of leisure industry businesses who reap hefty profits from tourism it might be wise to change the name 'shoulder season,' especially just before Christmas.

Foxy's Taboo

The Foxy Magic
Beautiful Location.
Al Fresco Dining, Cool Breezes
Mediterranean Fare with Flair
The Bubbly Pool Trail Starts Here

Free Giveaway
Bubbly Passion
(2 for 1)

Tel: 349-9250 • VHF: Ch 16 • www.foxysbar.com

Foxy's Taboo is the new 'In Place' to go for a delightful lunch or casual dinner. Their tag line says it all 'Mediterranean Fare with Flair'. Some of their tasty offerings include Taboo Salad, a special dish comprising beets, walnuts and gorgonzola cheese. There are also dishes like lamb, beef, chicken or shrimp shish kebabs, fish sandwiches, coconut rum shrimp, veggie pita and hummus as well as the ever popular burgers. One of the burgers is the sloop burger where a dollar of each one sold goes to the JVD Island Sloop Project, a part of the JVD Preservation Society's effort to teach the youth the island's heritage and involve them in the BVI's nautical past.

A visit to Foxy's Taboo should also be a precursor to a visit to the Bubbly Pool or a last stop for a refreshing pick-me-up. There's a dinghy dock and just offshore is a mooring field for overnight. Nearby is great snorkeling.

⊣ Cryptic Comment ⊢

My bank has a new service; they SMS you your balance. But I don't think they should add LOL at the end.

Specialty Drinks

Blue Taboo

Ingredients: 1 shot vodka
                 Peach Shnapps
                 1 shot Blue Curacao
                 Coco Lopez (cream of coconut)

Method: Blend all ingredients and serve over ice

Bubbly Passion

Ingredients: Passion Fruit Syrup
                 1 shot cognac
                 Top up with champagne

Method: Serve chilled. You'll want a second one of these.

Specialty Dish

Egg Plant Cheesecake

Ingredients: 2 Medium sized egg plants
                 1 Bulb of garlic
                 16oz Cream cheese
                 4 Whole eggs
                 1 Cup Marinara Sauce
                 Savoury Graham Cracker Crust for 9" pan

Method: Roast egg plant with garlic until soft (350 degree oven for 20
                 minutes). Puree in food processor. When cooled mix in cream
                 cheese, eggs and Marinara sauce. Pour mixture into crust and
                 bake in 350 degree oven for 60 minutes. Allow to cool for about
                 8 hours. Slice and serve with extra sauce and a sprinkling of
                 parmesan cheese. Can be warmed in microwave before serving.
                 (8 appetizer portions)

Foxy's Taboo

Foxy's Taboo

If you're feeling a little bit blue
Then grab some of your crew
Tell 'em the tale
Of the Bubbly Trail
But start with a drink at Taboo

When you get there jump right on in
You don't need a mask, snorkel or fin
The bubbles are fun
Soak up the sun
On your face, you'll have a big grin

**Why are married women heavier than single women?
Answer: Single women come home, look what's in the fridge and go to bed. Married women come home, look what's in the bed and go to the fridge.**

Ivan's Local Flavor

Ivan's Stress Free Bar

Thursday Night: Grand Barbecue Buffet
Live Reggae music by Jerry (Thursday)
New!! Holiday Apartments

Cabins, Tents and Tent Sites
Unique Shell Bar and Gift Shop. Moorings Available

Tel: 495-9358 • VHF: Ch 16
E mail: ivansstressfreeguesthouse@yahoo.com

Located on the sandy beach toward the east end of White Bay, Ivan's originated to serve campers in his campground adjacent to the bar. Now there are comfortable holiday apartments available to rent. The location soon became popular with the boating crowd because of its laid-back style, hammocks, honor bar and reasonably priced barbecue meals served on some evenings. Fresh fish is often on offer: Ivan is a fisherman in his rare moments of spare time.

It is a beach bar in the truest sense of the word: both interior and exterior are decorated with seashells in attractive designs and photographs of happenings and parties throughout the years and are displayed for all to see. On Thursdays during the season Reggae music by Jerry.

Many famous personalities and musicians have found Ivan's including Kenny Chesney, Keith Richard of the Rolling Stones, Dick Solberg and Willie Nelson. Some join the Ever Changing All Star International Band for an evening and make for an unforgettable time.

White Bay is a beautiful anchorage with crystal clear water and powdery sand but watch out for a ground sea if overnight anchoring is planned.

Specialty Drink

Ivan's Stress Free Punch

Ingredients:
2 teaspoons jelly from a female conch
1/2 cup water from a dildo cactus
Purée from one silly cybin mushroom
1/2 teaspoon of dried and powdered Billy goat scrotum
Finely diced bud of leatherback turtle

Method:
Mix all ingredients in a blender.
Pour over ice and garnish with grated iguana tail.

Note: It has been said that this unusual cocktail will put lead in your pencil. It will also aid in finding a place to put your pencil.

Specialty Dish

BBQ Buffet

Ivan's is famous for the Thursday Night Barbecue Buffet featuring freshly caught fish, sumptuous ribs and barbecued chicken. Eat under the tamarind tree overlooking White Bay. Ruben starts entertaining in the afternoon when visitors start arriving to enjoy cold drinks and great island music.

Cryptic Comment

Ladies, if a man says he will fix it, he will. No need to remind him every six months.

Ivan's Local Flavor

Ivan's Stress Free Bar

Ivan's Stress Free Bar

Located at pretty White Bay
At Ivan's they come to play
You came here once
To watch all the stunts
Now you're back for a stress free stay

The Stress Free Punch is a must
It's the drink of the upper crust
Is it an act?
Or a phrodisiac
Keep tryin' it till you go bust

Cryptic Comment

One day a handsome sailor asked a beautiful princess, "Will you marry me?" And she said, "No!" And he lived happily ever after -

He went sailing; watched all his favorite sports programs; picked up loose women, drank beer, had lots of money to spend and farted whenever he felt like it.

One Love

White Bay's Coolest Bar
Fresh Fish and Seafood Specials for Lunch
Rustic Bar, Toes in the Sand, Gift Shop
Live Reggae Music and Island Entertainment

Bushwacker (2 for 1)

Tel: 495-9829 • VHF Ch 16 • www.onelovebar.com

Seddy's One Love bar and lunch time restaurant has become a White Bay institution. Located at the western end of the beach you can't miss this unique bar decorated with fisherman's flotsam and jetsam. It's a true driftwood bar with fishing floats, lobster pots, nets etc. The bar is owned by Foxy's son, Seddy who seems to have inherited his dad's entertainment skills. Seddy's specialty is magic. You may be lucky enough to some amazing magic tricks - and if you want your kids to disappear, take 'em along.

The bar's specialty is the Bushwacker and as you can see from the recipe it packs quite a punch. The lunch menu is very popular with emphasis on fresh fish and seafood. Outside tables provide a great view, overlooking the beach and across to Tortola's north side.

On most days during the afternoon local musicians play island songs and reggae favorites. If you're lucky you might catch JVD's native son and guitar maestro, Ruben Chinnery. His repertoire is as long as the sky. If you like Johnny Cash request Fulsome Prison Blues, a classic!

| Cryptic Comment |

Behind every successful man is his woman. Behind the fall of a successful man is usually another woman.

Seddy's Bushwacker

Ingredients:
- 1 shot amber rum
- 1 shot vodka
- Coco Lopez
- Splash Bailey's Irish Cream
- Splash Kahlua
- Splash Amaretto

Method:
Mix all ingredients in a cocktail shaker or jug and pour over ice.
Garnish with a maraschino cherry

Lobster Quesadilla

Ingredients:
- Flour or Corn Tortlila
- Pre-cooked lobster chunks
- Onion
- Sweet Pepper
- Tomato
- Grated sharp cheddar cheese
- Olive Oil
- Salt and Pepper

Method:
Finely chop onion, pepper and tomato and sauté in frying pan until cooked, season to taste. Remove from frying pan.
Place tortilla in pan and flip several times until cooked. Layer the lobster and vegetable on tortilla and sprinkle cheese on top.
Fold in half and wait until cheese melts.
Serve with salad or appropriate garnish.

One Love

One Love

Seddy's is at White Bay
Where Ruben is known to play
Sing along
To an island song
It's likely to make your day

If you happen to be a back packer
At the bar, try their Bushwacker
You might have to teach
That duck on the beach
His name; he's known as the Quacker

In the bar you might find a Rasta
'No fish! So I'm just eatin' pasta'
Then a message of love
From the man up above
Said, 'Dem fish ain' swimmin' no fasta!'

**In order to prevent
herself from being called a flirt, she always
yielded easily.**

Sidney's Peace and Love

Free Giveaway Rum Punch (2 for 1)

Little Harbor's Premier Bar and Restaurant
Help Yourself Honor Bar

Giant Lobster Dinners, Fresh Fish
Fun filled Gift Shop

Tel: 495-9271 • VHF: Ch 16

Sidney's Peace and Love is tucked away in Jost van Dyke's Little Harbor. For all those whose wish it is to find local food, you've arrived. Sidney's has been catering to the yachting crowd since 1982.

Moorings are available in the anchorage and when you've tied your boat up securely head to the dock where Janet or Strawberry will be there to help you ashore. Then head to the self service bar and mix yourself a drink, as strong or weak as you like.

The menu is local, with lobster, fresh fish, conch, barbecued ribs, chicken and more. Meals are served with a delicious home-made cole slaw, buttery sweet corn on the cob, potato salad, fried plantain and rice and beans. No, you won't go hungry here.

The gift shop is usually packed with island gifts and souvenirs. Hats and sarongs are perhaps the best sellers but you may find something unique here. Sometimes people buy a new T shirt and leave their old one hanging from the ceiling, scrawled with a message of rum induced wisdom.

Cryptic Comment

A clear conscience is usually the sign of a bad memory.

Specialty Drink

You name it, cos you're going to mix it!

Ingredients: Dark rum
                 Light rum
                 More rum
                 Then some

Method: Pour over ice with a twist of lime. Sit down before drinking

Specialty Dish

Lobster, Boiled & Grilled

Boiled   Boiled lobster is often the preferred method. A lobster is taken live from the pen. It is immersed in a large pot of boiling water and simmered for about ten minutes. Then it is removed and sliced lengthwise. Seasonings are added and then the half shell lobster is painted with butter and grilled on medium heat coals till just golden at the edges. It is served with melted butter and fresh lime wedge.

Grilled   The lobster is sliced in half lengthwise, painted with melted butter, seasoned and wrapped in foil. The lobster halves are cooked in their own juices on the grill for about fifteen minutes. They are served with lime wedges and melted butter.

Cryptic Comment

**What's the difference
between a Porsche and a porcupine?
The porcupine has the pricks on the outside.**

Sidney's Peace and Love

Sidney's Peace and Love

Sidney's is famous for food
From the sea, fresh lobster, it's good
Served with a smile
Caribbean style
It'll put you in a good mood

Their shop is one of the best
Think peace and love, not stress
There's colorful clothes
Yep, I'll take one of those
Then I'll be the best dressed

Cryptic Comment

**Everyone's a genius,
but if you judge a fish by its ability to climb a
tree it will live its whole life believing it's stupid.**

Soggy Dollar Bar

Home of the 'Original Painkiller'
Popular Award Winning Beach Bar

Free Giveaway Painkiller

Casual Lunches
Gourmet Candlelit Dinners
Great Gift Shop

Tel: 495-9888 • www.soggydollar.com

The White Bay Sandcastle is the name of the little resort that incorporates the famous Soggy Dollar Bar. They are both little changed from the way they were in 1971 when George Myrick opened the now famous beach resort, except that the volume of traffic has increased a hundredfold; and by traffic I mean boat traffic. The sandy beach at White Bay rises steeply to the palm trees so the beach is visible from quite a distance, hence the name. The texture of the sand is particularly fine, almost powdery, and this is largely the result of a substantial fringing reef. Between beach and reef is crystal clear turquoise water about 8-ft deep and perfect for anchoring when there's no ground sea. Once anchored the beach is so inviting that many people jump in and swim straight to the beach and then walk on up to the bar – with wet money to buy drinks. Hey presto! The Soggy Dollar Bar. It's probably the only bar with a clothesline with wet dollars hanging out to dry.

The bar is very casual – people look at you askance if you're wearing shoes. Lounge chairs and hammocks are provided for patrons and if you succumb to more than one of their famous Painkillers you can try your skills at a variety of bar games and puzzles like the ring game, nail puzzle or Jenga. It's the perfect spot for a cheeseburger in paradise, but the more adventurous might try a chicken roti. Reservations requested by 4 p.m. for their gourmet, four course, candlelit dinner in the open-air, beach front restaurant.

Specialty Drink

Painkiller

Ingredients: Pusser's Dark Rum
                Coco Lopez (Coconut Cream)
                Orange Juice
                Pineapple Juice
                Grated Nutmeg

Method: Mix all liquid ingredients in a blender, pour over ice cubes, sprinkle
                with grated nutmeg and garnish with a cherry. You'll need more
                than one of these.

Note: *The Soggy Dollar Bar invented this popular Caribbean Drink.*
                The exact proportions are kept secret but be sure this will be the
                best Painkiller you will ever taste. Experiment with the proportions
                a little until you get the mixture you like.
                (tip: more pineapple than orange).

Specialty Dish

Chicken Roti

Chicken Roti is a Caribbean classic. Pre-cooked chunks of tender chicken in a
curry sauce are combined with pieces of boiled potato and chick peas (garbanzo
beans). The mixture is placed onto a West Indian flat bread the size of a dinner
plate and folded into a small square pie. The Soggy Dollar serves it with a salad
dressed with a balsamic vinaigrette.

Soggy Dollar Bar

Soggy Dollar Bar

It's on a beach called White Bay
A place where the world comes to play
You can see from afar
The Soggy Dollar Bar
Go there, have fun, make your day

They have awards for best bar
That makes them the bar with a star
I have a hunch
You'll go there for lunch
Like pirates 'n sailors, oh Aaaarhh!

Today's City Dweller:

Get up while it's still dark; get the kids up by threat and force. High pitched orders and responses at almost scream level. Run to the car with coffee in plastic cup and shoelaces still undone. Drive for two minutes and then join the queue in the traffic jam. Get the finger for pushing in. Arrive at office five minutes late, nowhere to park. Drive around the block once, finally find a spot but narrowly lose it to dork in law office next door.

Arrive in office half an hour late, get shouted at by boss.

Open mail and find 1) A summons for unpaid speeding ticket. 2) Complaint for sexual harassment – you happened to bump into fat, unattractive coffee woman. 3) Warning for not implementing required fire drill. 4) Fees that you earned are being challenged by dork from competing law office. 5) Results from doctor's office saying your blood pressure is high, cholesterol level is dangerous and you're on the road for a stroke. Reminder that your colonoscopy is scheduled for next week. 6) Letter from the IRS. You're being audited at an unspecified time within next two weeks. "Better to fess up now," it says.

You work hard all day, miss lunch and leave office at 9pm. Find two wheels missing from your car. "Please drive to police station to file a report," says desk sergeant.

Charlie, the Cruising Sailor:

Get up to magical sunrise, enjoy coffee in the cockpit while listening to 'Easy morning music' on FM. Write 'to do' list during second cup and watch hot babes on next boat going skinny dipping. Dinghy ashore to buy warm croissants, French bread and tropical fruit for late breakfast. Spend morning doing chores on board: a little varnishing, tune up outboard, pump up dinghy. Test outboard and when hot babe waves, you maneuver over to their boat and have a chat. Afternoon sail with snorkeling trip arranged. Short close reach to Palm Tree Island. Enjoy snorkeling in sparkling clear water and watching amazing reef action – and hot babes snorkeling. Try to start engine but it fails to start. Oh dear, babes will have to stay the night on board; they don't mind at all. Fix dynamite Planter's Punches. After second round one hot babe complains of sunburn and Charlie, ever the chivalrous host, volunteers to massage it better with jelly from Aloe Vera plant he just happens to have on board. Other hot babe becomes jealous; needs massaging too. After a third round they all end up in a pile on Charlie's queen size fore peak berth. No sign of the IRS.

The Trip to Italy

A young New York woman was so depressed that she decided to end her life by throwing herself into the ocean; but just before she could throw herself from the docks, a handsome young man stopped her.

"You have so much to live for," said the man. "I'm a sailor, and we are off to Italy tomorrow. I can stow you away on my ship. I'll take care of you, bring you food every day, and keep you happy."

With nothing to lose, combined with the fact that she had always wanted to go to Italy , the woman accepted.

That night the sailor brought her aboard and hid her in a small but comfortable compartment in the ship's hold.

From then on, every night he would bring her three sandwiches, a bottle of red wine, and make love to her until dawn.

Three weeks later she was discovered by the captain during a routine inspection.

"What are you doing here?" asked the captain.

"I have an arrangement with one of the sailors," she replied. "He brings me food and I get a free trip to Italy ."

"I see," the captain says.

Then her conscience got the best of her, and she added, "Plus, he's screwing me."

"He certainly is," replied the captain. "This is the Staten Island Ferry."

The Bath and Turtle's
Rendezvous Bar

**Beautiful Setting by the Boats
at VG Yacht Harbor
Favored by Locals and Tourists alike**

Free Giveaway Rum Punch with Lunch

**Live Band on Wednesdays,
 Caribbean BBQ Buffet
Sunday Afternoon Live Music, Party Atmosphere
Large TVs for Sporting Events
Breakfast, Lunch and Dinner. Free Wi Fi**

**Tel: 495-5752 • VHF: Ch 16 • E mail: bathandturtle@surfbvi.com
Web Site: www.bathandturtle.com**

The Bath and Turtle; it's a catchy name you're not likely to forget. The name refers to the BVI's natural wonder, the Baths, while turtles are a part of the islands' prolific sea life.

The Rendezvous Bar is the latest addition to the Bath and Turtle and is located right on the marina's water-front. Enjoy the cool breezes while checking out the boats coming and going. It's the perfect spot for lunch or a happy hour drink in this relaxing al fresco setting. All the pub fare is available, from fish and chips, burgers, pizzas right through to the local favorite, Caribbean roti with mango chutney.

On Sunday afternoons a scratch band provides entertainment so make this a stop for a fun afternoon. On Wednesday evenings a Caribbean barbecue buffet is served and a live band plays for your listening or dancing pleasure. This is a popular evening event so come early.

Specialty Drink

Rum Boogie

Ingredients: 1 shot amber rum
1 shot Triple Sec
1 shot Amaretto
Squeeze of fresh lim
Touch of Coca Cola

Method: Mix all the ingredients in a shaker except the Coke.
Pour into a tall glass over ice cubes and top up with the Coke.
Garnish with a maraschino cherry, wedge of lime and a
slice of orange

Specialty Dish

BBQ

The Bath and Turtle's Rendezvous Bar serves up a delicious Caribbean barbecue buffet on Wednesday evenings.

Cryptic Comment

**It's lonely at the top,
but you do eat better.**

The Bath and Turtle's
Rendezvous Bar

The Bath and Turtle's Rendezvous Bar

A turtle is taking a bath
In the sea, right by the path
That big round shell
Is giving him hell
Everyone's having a laugh

On the deck enjoy a cold beer
There's nothing that could be more clear
You are a boatie
So order a roti
Just relax, there's nothing to fear

Diplomacy is the art of letting someone else get your way.

The
Bitter End Yacht Club
and Crawl Pub

Best Water Sports Resort in the World
Sports Bar with Darts, Pool, Foosball
Draft Beer on Tap, Build your own Pizza
Big Screen TVs. Projector with Giant Screen
11am to 10pm. Great Pub Food

Tel: 494-3152 • VHF: Quarterdeck Marina • Ch 16
www.beyc.com

The Bitter End Yacht Club is widely seen as the finest water sports resort in the Caribbean and arguably the world. Its location on a protected shore of North Sound, Virgin Gorda, facing the setting sun is nothing less than perfect. Its close proximity to Eustatia Sound, an abundance of coves, sandy beaches and coral reefs attests to its magnificent setting.

Dining options at the Bitter End include a pub, a pool service and two restaurants. The Clubhouse Steak & Seafood Grill is Bitter End's landmark restaurant, featuring generous buffets and table service for breakfast, lunch and dinner as well as cocktail service on the terrace all day and evening. For over 30 years, it's been a favorite rendezvous for visiting boaters and famished resort guests alike.

The Almond Walk features al fresco dining various days of the week. Guests enjoy lavish themed gourmet buffets and live music by local musicians.

The Crawl Pub is home to a brick oven delivering the best homemade pizza in the Caribbean. The Pub menu offers casual dining for lunch and dinner, as well as a full service bar and entertainment each week.

An entire day can be pleasantly spent by the pool with a light curried salad for lunch. Seafood and lobster dishes are also available and cocktails are served during early evening hours

Specialty Drink

Tropical Punch

Ingredients: 1 shot Mount Gay Rum
Grapefruit Juice
Squeeze of fresh lime
Splash of Ginger Beer
Dash of Angostura Bitters

Method: Pour all ingredients over ice cubes, stir and garnish with a cherry
and a slice of lime

Specialty Dish

Mahi-Mahi

At the Steak and Seafood Grill the restaurant boasts the freshest fish in North
Sound from 'Sea to Table.' One of the most popular dishes in the restaurant is
the Pecan/Ginger Crusted Mahi Mahi. It is served over a curried pumpkin risotto
and accompanied by a home-made mango/raisin chutney.

Cryptic Comment

**I don't suffer from insanity,
I enjoy every moment of it.**

The Bitter End Yacht Club and Crawl Pub

The Bitter End Yacht Club and Crawl Pub

If your wish is to live in hi style
The Bitter End's the best by a mile
The tasty food
Is ever so good
Shall I give you the number to dial

Or just dinghy to their great pub
It's the home of really good grub
An oven made pizza
Should do more than just please her
Then back to the boat for some love

Cryptic Comment

"I am enclosing two
tickets to the first night of my new play;
bring a friend, if you have one."
George Bernard Shaw to Winston Churchill.

"Cannot possibly attend
first night, will attend second ... if there is one."

Fat Virgin Café

"Big Drinks, Great Food, No Shoes"

Bistro Dining on the Waterfront at Biras Creek

Island Dishes, Rotis, Sandwiches, Salads

Fresh Fish, Burgers and More.
New: Giant Bruschettas, Conch Fritters

Tel: 495-7052 • VHF: Ch 16 • www.fatvirgin.com

The Fat Virgin Café opened its doors in 1999 and became an instant success. In an area of luxury resorts, expensive eateries and fine dining this 'bistro' style establishment found a steady stream of customers. The location, right at the water's edge, is very Caribbean and the service is friendly and efficient. The café can only be accessed by water and boaters can dinghy right up to the bistro, tie up and sit at a table. Land based guests can take the Biras Creek ferry straight to the dock.

The food specials include tender guava glazed baby back ribs, boneless Caribbean chicken roti, grilled wahoo, pan fried snapper, burgers, fritters and homemade soup. Homemade thick cut fries are also popular as is the Cole Slaw.

Another reason to visit the Fat Virgin is to browse the chic island boutique, Treasures. You'll discover original Caribbbean handicrafts such as metal sculptures, pottery, moko jumbie dolls, stained glass, books, maps and table accessories. You'll also find stylish, casual clothing and beachwear, including sarongs, sandals, and designer swimsuits. Gorgeous handcrafted earrings and necklaces make perfect accent pieces for fashionable dresses, tunics and wrapskirts. If you want a Biras Creek or Fat Virgin souvenir to bring home, select a shirt, cap or other collectible. We even have a selection of toiletries and sundries in case you forgot something at home. This is not some island gift shop but a boutique where careful buying offers a unique selection of jewelry, gifts and souvenirs.

Specialty Drink

The Virgin

Ingredients: Puree of Blood Orange
                Elderflower Liqueur

Method: This unique drink is simply made by combining the ingredients
                and pouring over ice. The cocktail is garnished with a slice of
                orange and a cherry

Specialty Dishes

Bruschetta

The Fat Virgin is offering its Giant Bruschetta as a new appetizer. It requires a
long baguette sliced lengthwise, spread with a special tomato sauce and grilled
with Mozarella until melted. Served warm.

The Fat Virgin is very proud of its conch fritters, which become more popular
every year. They are served with their own homemade remoulade sauce.

Cryptic Comment

**"I've just learned about
his illness. Let's hope it's nothing trivial."**

Fat Virgin Café

"Big Drinks, Great Food, No Shoes"

Fat Virgin Café

It's a bistro called The Fat Virgin
Customers dem need no urgin'
Here there's a dish
Of local fresh fish
Time for a bit of real splurgin'

They serve up the food with a smile
The conch fritters are best – by a mile!
A West Indian Roti
Suits every boaty
Then you'll have a smile on your dial

Cryptic Comment

**Knowledge is
knowing a tomato is a fruit.
Wisdom is not putting it in a fruit salad.**

Jumbies Bar at Leverick Bay

Michael Beans' Happy Aaaarh Show
  (in season)
Friday Night Beach Party.
  BBQ, Live Music, Mocko Jumbie Dancers
Free Showers and Wi Fi,
  (Free ice and water with mooring or dockage receipt).
Great Beach Bar Menu
Fine Dining Upstairs
  ($25 discount 4 or more with mooring or dockage discount).

Tel: 340-3005 • Ch 16 (Marina)
www.Leverick Bay.com

Situated at Leverick Bay and nestled into a small natural cove the restaurant/bar is the centerpiece of a beautifully designed mini village of shops and service oriented businesses.

There is a boat rental, scuba center, coffee shop, cyber café as well as a Laundromat, Spa, grocery shop and quality gift shops. From here there is road access to the rest of Virgin Gorda.

The attractive beach bar, "Jumbies" is delighting visitors and locals alike. Situated on the sand with attractive gazebos this facility features special evening events with the highlight being the 'Happy Aaaarh show with Michael Beans. Beans' show is pirate themed and audience participation is encouraged. The conch blowing contest is hugely popular with a special section for the kids. On Friday nights there's a sumptuous 'all –you-can-eat ' buffet with a live band for dancing. After dinner mocko jumbies entertain with acrobatic antics.

The staff at Leverick Bay is hell bent on providing an extremely high standard of food and service. Friendly and attentive service is the rule rather than the exception here. There's a mini market, which is called "The Chef's Pantry." The food store has a good selection of deli goods and quality meats and fish so that boats and villas can provision from a professional chef's kitchen.

The Restaurant at Leverick Bay is a delightful dinnertime eatery with central bar and tables on the veranda overlooking the sound. Downstairs a poolside bar and restaurant serves pizza, sandwiches, fish and chips and burgers at lunchtime and your favorite tropical drink can be enjoyed while lounging by the freshwater pool.

Note: Beans' show is on Monday to Thursday – 5 to 7pm, January to May

Specialty Drink

Bushwacker

Ingredients:	1 shot Amber Rum
	1 shot Vodka
	1 shot Khalua
	1 shot Amaretto
	1 shot Bailey's
	Coco Lopez to taste
Method:	Mix ingredients in a blender and serve over ice

Specialty Dish

Fish 'n Chips

Ingredients and method: Season tender fingers of mahi-mahi fish. Prepare a batter of cornstarch, flour and eggs and season with salt and pepper. Add cornflakes and Japanese bread crumbs. Dip the fish into batter mixture and coat thoroughly. Deep fry in hot oil. The chips should be blanched i.e. cooked but not browned and kept ready. Finish by cooking to a golden brown.

Jumbies Bar at Leverick Bay

Jumbies Bar at Leverick Bay

Leverick Bay on some days
Plays host to the mocko jumbies
With very long legs
Like wooden pegs
Some say they're African zombies

They put on a hell of a show
After the buffet, you know
There's roasted meats
And West Indian treats
Enough for a tropical glow

The show is right on the sand
Reggae is played by the band
After some rum
You want to have fun
But she'd rather relax and be fanned

Cryptic Comment

I told my family 'I don't want to be in a vegetative state, attached to a machine with fluids being poured into my system. Well, they shut down my computer, threw my wine down the sink and made me go for a walk... the bastards!

Saba Rock

Tiny Island Paradise.
Free ice and water for yachtsmen.
Mini Aquarium, Gift Shop/Museum

Free Giveaway
2 for 1 Mai Tai

NEW! Over-the-Water Deck, Manicured Gardens,
Comfortable Rooms with Special Boaters Rates
Excellent Food and Friendly Staff
Happy Hour and Fish Feeding, Underwater Lights

Tel: 495-7711 • VHF: Ch 16 • www.sabarock.com

Saba Rock is located in Virgin Gorda's North Sound. It's a paradise isle housing a popular restaurant and bar with over-the-water seating. Saba Rock has many unique attractions; a mini museum/gift shop, an aquarium with nautical arti-facts from some of the BVI's shipwrecks, beautiful manicured gardens with a NEW over-the-water deck looking out over panoramic Eustatia Sound and a sandy beach area with hammocks. The resort has eight delightful rooms with most overlooking North Sound. They advertise 'Unlimited hot water and over a hundred TV channels.' If you wish to come by private yacht the marina has slips available. If you're land based give them a shout and they'll come and pick you up by ferry.

The restaurant is extremely popular and many visitors come for the happy hour fish feeding, a delight for the kids. After a cocktail or tropical drink many stay for dinner taking advantage from either the bar menu or the full restaurant menu with salad bar buffet and hot buffet as well as a full a la carte menu. Dur-ing holiday times a full, all-you-can-eat buffet is offered with a roast meat sta-tion.

The island now boasts two fabulous locations (the new deck or sand beach) for private dinner parties, full moon get-togethers, birthday celebrations, anniversaries, weddings and special events. You will be allocated your own staff, a barbecue can be set up for your choice of steaks, fish, lobster... or you name it. Iced champagne can be brought out in buckets... The possibilities are endless. Several days notice will be needed for this service.

Specialty Drink

Mai Tai

Ingredients: 2 shots white rum
1 shot Curacao
1 oz sweet and sour mix (simple syrup and lime juice)
2 oz pineapple juice
1 shot Myer's rum (as floater)

Method: Reserve the Myer's rum. Mix all other ingredients together in a shaker with ice. Pour over ice cubes and finish with a floater of the Myer's rum. Garnish with a wedge of lime and a maraschino cherry

Specialty Dish

Fish Tacos

Fresh mahi-mahi is cooked to tender perfection. Taco shells are cooked to order. The fish is layered into the taco shell. Finely chopped onion, shredded lettuce, chopped tomato and grated cheddar cheese are loaded onto the warm taco shell and the whole thing is finished with their home-made taco sauce. Three of these are served per portion and accompanied by Saba Rock' s famous, seasoned shoe-string fries.

Saba Rock

Saba Rock

It looks like a paradise isle
So quaint and always in style
The gardens out back
There's nothing they lack
They're beautiful, best by a mile

Go into their unique gift shop
It's the best, the cream of the crop
Buy a new cap
Or a sailor's hat
Then into the bar for a drop

There's a 'special' on the price of a room
Your girlfriend will want one quite soon
"I'm off that old boat
It's hardly afloat
And I'm really not feeling in tune."

Cryptic Comment

If you stumble,
make it part of the dance

Top of the Baths

The Top of the Baths is located above one of the most famous beaches in the world, The Baths, on Virgin Gorda in the British Virgin Islands. The Baths is one of the most well-known and popular landmarks in the British Virgin Islands. Gigantic granite boulders and half-submerged rocks line the southern seashore of Virgin Gorda, creating natural sculptures, grottos, tunnels, and arches - a wonderful place to swim, snorkel, and explore. Sandy beaches are lined with coconut palms, adding to the dramatic effect.

The Top of the Baths is a delightful bar and restaurant just a short walk from the entrance to the famous trail through the boulders. The panoramic view from their deck is nothing short of spectacular. The fresh water pool can be used to cool off before popping that ice cold beer. There are shops here too, so browse on through. You just might find that perfect gift for those unlucky souls back home.

Cryptic Comment

"You shut your mouth when you're talking to me."

Specialty Drink

Boulder Roller

Ingredients:
- Dark & light rum
- Tequila
- Gin
- Vodka
- Orange juice
- Pineapple juice
- Grenadine.

Method: Stir all ingredients together and serve in a large cocktail glass over ice. Garnish with a slice of lime. Guaranteed to have you singing a ll the way back to your boat.

Specialty Dish

Crispy Chicken Spring Roll

Ingredients:
- 1/2 lb cooked chicken
- 2 carrots shredded or cut into fine strips
- 1/2 cabbage shredded
- Vegetable oil for deep frying
- 3 tbs flour, water for making paste
- Salt and pepper to taste
- Secret plum dipping sauce
- Pre-prepared spring roll wraps

Method: Heat a small amount of the oil and stir fry cabbage and carrots. Add the chicken and toss the mixture with some of the plum sauce to make filling. Season to taste. Lay out the wraps and fill with 2 tbs of filling. Roll the spring rolls tightly and seal the edges using the flour and water paste. Heat the oil in a deep fryer until very hot. Fry rolls until golden brown and serve with plum dipping sauce.

Top of the Baths

Top of the Baths

The Baths on a beautiful beach
Are truly within easy reach
Don't wait till you're older
To check out the boulders
Dinghy over, into the breech

Take the trail up to the top
There's a bar, a pool, make a stop
Then take in the view
A fantastic blue
Without doubt the cream of the crop

Cryptic Comment

I didn't attend the funeral,
but I sent a nice letter saying I approved of it."

The question of how to find a good crew for an offshore yacht passage can often be a vexing one. There are several avenues down which a sailor can search; web sites, classified sections of nautical publications, notice boards and personal recommendations. Web sites usually have large listings of competent crew but applicants normally expect payment and agencies want commissions. Classifieds can be confusing by their often ambiguous and tempting lingo. Here's an example: 'Young adventurous female desires crew placement on sailing yacht; very experienced in many positions and loves skinny dipping. Can cook, clean, steer the boat and take orders from the most demanding captain.' The wannabe crew will likely receive a lot of replies but the eventual captain may soon be disillusioned when he finds an overweight, middle-aged divorcee and recently discovered lesbian lounging around his salon and eating all his supplies before throwing up all over the cabin sole.

Of course captains can be equally devious. One penniless shipwrecked captain I once knew placed the following advertisement in a sailing magazine: 'Experienced world sailor, navigator, and qualified captain seeks female boat owner for relationship. Please send photo...of boat.'

Charlie has seen a business opportunity here and has decided to start a web site, Wikicrew. Actually it started out as WickedCrew but was shortened. There are several sub-headings like Sailing Yachts, Racing Boats, Stink Pots, Super Stink Pots, Merchant Ships and Cattle Boats. If you want a job on a cruise ship go to the latter; a gas guzzling carbon foot printer, then go to Super Stink Pots. You get the idea? Then there are sub sub-headings like: good cook, can't cook, deck apes, bow candy, romance, sex no strings, share expenses, work for passage, sex for passage, sex back passage (homosexuals). The idea is to get all the worrisome maybes, mightbes and couldbes out of the way before heading out to sea. Every applicant must provide full length photos, both head on and profile so no-one is disappointed. Once a handsome, muscle bound deck ape type sent a head and shoulders picture to a lonely female sail boat captain; she was immediately seduced but later somewhat shocked when she discovered he had no legs (a happy ending here: he wasn't incapacitated in any other area and in fact turned out to be a wizard in the rather cramped engine room).

Lately Charlie has been seeing dollar signs; he is so convinced Wikicrew will be a success. He is now contemplating an interactive web site, Crewbook: the sharing of nautical adventures, likes and dislikes of crew members, fetishes, fancies and friggin' in the riggin,' all on video link. Boom! The sky's the limit.

Toes in the Sand

It is no wonder that the Virgin Islands are recognized as the sailing capital of the world. There are so many beautiful and protected anchorages in close proximity, so many beach bars and great restaurants, a proliferation of protected coral reefs for diving and snorkeling and many trails for hiking. Add to this a 'treasure island,' a geological wonder, 'the Baths,' an atoll like island, Anegada and an island named after a pirate, Jost van Dyke. 'If people can't have a good time in the VI they can't have a good time anywhere,' explains Charlie with a smile. Then he tries to ascertain what type of cruise his guests would like: laid back at quiet anchorages, party every night, fine dining or barbecue on the boat.

One of Charlie's recent charter parties was particularly fond of adult beverages, happy hours of laughter and dinner out. One beautiful night out at the Anegada Reef Hotel we were enjoying a wonderful dinner beachside, toes in the sand, when the subject of boat names came up. The lady, Betty, somewhat tipsy, said that she was going to name their new boat Toes in the Sand after the incredible night they were enjoying. Husband Joe agreed but thought it might be a tad long so Charlie intervened and suggested the acronym. It took a few seconds but eventually a few chuckles broke through except that Betty had turned slightly red and was attempting to change the subject. It was then that Charlie noticed that she was rather flat chested and that perhaps he'd made a snafu (another acronym for Situation Normal, All Fucked Up).

Joe thought that the idea of an acronym for a boat's name was a winner. For the rest of the meal he kept coming up with ideas. "What about Sailing Into Stormy Seas?" No that might evoke the wrath of Poseidon. "What about Tropical Islands Please Salty Yachtsmen?" Charlie thought this might be appropriate since Joe had just ordered a third bottle of wine. By this time Betty was getting right into the swing of things and in fact had come round to the idea of Toes in the Sand. Then Joe came up with Navigating under Tropical Skies and everyone agreed this was a winner.

So if you see a boat out there in the next few months called Tits and Nuts you'll know the origin of the name – and you can blame Charlie and the sandy beach outside the Anegada Reef Hotel.

Anegada Reef Hotel

Starlit Dinners on the Sand
Reservations by 4pm
Famous for Barbecued Lobster
  Direct from the Pen
Rum Smoothies
Interesting Gift Shop

Free Giveaway Famous Rum Smoothie

Tel: 495-8002 • VHF: Ch 16 • www.anegadareef.com
E Mail: info@anegadareef.com

Anegada Reef Hotel is Anegada's only hotel. Located at Setting Point it is the centre of activity for yachtsmen and the occasional visitor to this unique and sparsely populated island. You can sense the difference when you approach the island by boat: the bases of the fleecy cumulus are tinged with turquoise and trees seem to grow out of the water on the horizon. The tallest point on Anegada is 28-ft.

Visitors come here for two main reasons: to sample the island's abundant lobsters and to snorkel some of the best underwater scenery in the Virgin Islands, off the north shore beaches. But there is something else Anegada gives to the itinerant visitor: a feeling of carefree abandon of almost dreamlike quality and a humility that large expanses of simple beauty can evoke... until you come back to reality with a "milk of amnesia" and a huge plate of baked lobster dripping with melted butter.

The small hotel/ bar/ restaurant has been running for nearly 20 years. The open-air dining area is just behind the sandy beach in a delightful tropical setting and breakfast lunch and dinner are available. If no one's around just help yourself from the bar and start a tab. A regular shuttle bus will take you to the north side beaches.

Specialty Drink

Milk of Amnesia

Ingredients: 1 shot Vodka
                1 shot Kahlua
                1 shot Amaretto
                Milk

Method: Mix all ingredients in a cocktail shaker. Pour over ice cubes and finish with freshly grated nutmeg

Specialty Dish

Whole Grilled Lobster

The Anegada Reef Hotel is renowned for its fresh grilled lobster.
The lobsters are brought straight from the pen, are then bisected and painted liberally with melted butter. They are then wrapped in foil and grilled on the open air grills made from 55 gallon drums, home style with local wood to add that unique flavor.

Baby Back Pork Ribs are also very popular. These are par boiled in the hotel's special seasoning. Then they are liberally painted with homemade barbecue sauce and grilled to perfection. Yum!

Cryptic Comment

I've only been wrong once, and that was when I thought I was wrong

Anegada Reef Hotel

Anegada Reef Hotel

Their lobster has given them fame
In a dish with a popular name
It's called a crustacean
An impossible temptation
With butter, it's the name of the game

Some ribs might be to your taste
The chef will liberally baste
Them with bbq sauce
Which may be the cause
Of an increasing size to your waist

In the long run,
we're all fertilizer, that's a guarantee.

But while we're alive we should remember:
Happiness is a gift we give ourselves.
Being nice and kindhearted wins out and going
the extra mile pays off. Simplicity is the key to a
good life. Time is more important than money
because the best things in life are free.

The Big Bamboo

**Self Catering Cottages on the Beach
   at Loblolly Bay
Spectacular Beach, Hammocks and
   Palapas, Great Snorkeling
Fantastic Beach Bar, Island Style Lunches,
   Ice Cream Bar, Gift Shop
Dinner. Reservations Required by 4pm. Free Transportation**

**Tel: 495-8129 • Cell: 499-1680 (beach) • VHF: Ch 16.
E mail: bigbamboovillas@gmail.com**

Free Giveaway
Bamboo Teaser
(2 for 1)

On the north side of Anegada on one of the BVI's most beautiful beaches, Loblolly Bay, you will find the Big Bamboo. Today the Big Bamboo is more than just a beach bar. The famous restaurant and beach bar has added several self catering cottages with cooking and maid services on request. A gift shop with the addition of basic foodstuffs, ice cream parlor, snorkeling and dive services all combine to make the Big Bamboo a self contained mini resort. Anegada has long been a 'must stop' destination for yachtsmen and a steady stream of visitors arrive daily by open-air mini bus from the anchorage. The sweeping sandy beach and excellent snorkeling add to the Big Bamboo's attractive location. Shady hammocks under the sea grape trees or palapas provide for perfect relaxation while sipping a tropical cocktail from the beach bar. Fresh fish and shellfish are specialties on the lunch menu and starlit dinners are offered with free transportation to and from the anchorage. The bar has some of the most imaginative drink specials on the island. One is the Anegada Davida named for the famous rock song of the 70s by the Iron Butterfly. It's a shortened form of 'In the garden of Eden.' Say it quickly and you'll see.

Bamboo Teaser

Ingredients:
1 shot Myers Dark Rum
1 shot Kahlua
A mixture of fruit juices

Method:
Mix or shake together and pour over ice cubes.

Anegada Davida

Ingredients:
This cocktail is secret but contains an assortment of exotic liqueurs. These are mixed with lychees or Chinese gooseberries and blended with crushed ice.
You'll probably want a second round!

Specialty Dish

Grilled Whole Lobster

This Anegada specialty is served with melted butter and a squeeze of fresh lime juice.

The Big Bamboo

The Big Bamboo

I asked my lady what should I do,
To make her happy not make her blue
She said, "The only thing I want from you,
Is a little bit of de big bamboo."

I sold my lady a banana plant
She said, "I like it, he elegant
We shouldn't let he go to waste
But he's much too soft to suit my taste."

She met a China man, Him Hung Low
They got married, went to Mexico
But she divorced him very quick
She said, "I want bamboo, not chopstick."

Cryptic Comment

If you get an email telling you that you can catch Swine Flu from cans of ham then delete it. It's Spam.

Neptune's Treasure

**"Freshest Fish in the BVI,
  Because We Catch It"**
"Huge Lobster Dinners"
Breakfast, Lunch and Dinner
Family Run Guest House with AC Rooms
Pam's Bakery on Site.

Tel: 495-9439 • VHF: Ch 16

*Star Giveaway
Bottle of Wine
with Dinner
(1 per table of 4)*

Neptune's Treasure is a family success story unmatched in the BVI. Vernon and Julie Soares, of Portuguese descent, came to the BVI from Bermuda in the late 60s and began a fishing business in Jost van Dyke. It wasn't long before they realized that the best fishing was in Anegada and Neptune's Treasure was born. The primary fishing was longlining for swordfish and soon the family was supplying the whole of the BVI. In 1973 a small bar was established on the property at Setting Point and a restaurant soon followed – serving mostly seafood, of course. Now there's a guesthouse, an expanded bar and restaurant with deck, a bakery and a successful fishing business continues.

Every year Neptune's Treasure hosts the Dark and Stormy race weekend which takes place in March as a fun weekend with informal racing from Tortola to Anegada and back and a rest and relaxation day in between with all kinds of beach games and side trips.

By 2013 an expanded menu was put in place with such delights as Mark's homemade smoked pate, coconut cracked conch, and peppered shrimp for appetizers. Soups include Anegada seafood chowder and a chilled Gazpacho. Besides their famous lobster, entrées include swordfish, mahi-mahi and wahoo cooked how you like with a variety of sauces of your choice. Other items include duck, ribeye steak and ginger chicken. Neptune's Treasure now has the best selection of dishes on Anegada.

Pam's bakery is now inside the restaurant building. She makes the scrumptious dinner time desserts such as Key Lime Pie and chocolate brownies. From 7am fresh breads and baguettes are available as well as banana bread and cinnamon rolls – still warm from the oven! Delish!

Specialty Drinks

Dark & Stormy

Ingredients: 1 shot Goslings rum in an 8-ounce glass
Top up with Barritts ginger beer

Method: Pour over ice cubes. Floater of Gosling's rum (optional)
Note: This is a Bermuda classic

Anegada Sunset

Ingredients: 1 shot peach schnapps
1 shot Grand Marnier
1/2 ounce Grenadine
2 ounces orange juice

Method: Mix well together and pour over ice cubes.
Garnish with a maraschino cherry

Specialty Dish

Lobster

Neptune's Treasure is famous for its grilled lobster. The lobster is par boiled and then finished under the grill with melted butter

Neptune's Treasure

Neptune's Treasure

The treasure here's from Neptune
Better visit real soon
It could be some fish
Or a conch dish
Come in March, May or in June

Bring a good thirst when you come
In order to have some fine rum
With ginger beer
You'll have to steer...
Back to the bar for more fun

Come early in the morning
You awake, or feelin' a bit grim
A cinnamon roll
Or breakfast in a bowl
Then off to the beach for limin'

Cryptic Comment

**When my wife gives me the
'silent treatment' She thinks it's a punishment!**

Pirates Bight

Lunch and dinner
Deck chairs on the beach
Gift Shop
After dinner party nightly

Tel: 496 7827 • VHF: CH 16
www.normanislandpirates.com

At the head of the bay in Norman Island's Bight is the party bar and restaurant called Pirates' Bight. By day it's the favorite of the day excursion boats who often stop for lunch and drinks after snorkeling adventures or hiking over the island in search of buried treasure.

The Treasure Caves are a big attraction here: A chest of treasure was found in the southern most cave in 1910 and the finder became rich because of it. A bunch of English scallywags seized a shipload of treasure from a foundering Spanish galleon off a storm ravaged coast in North Carolina in 1750. A large part of it found its way to Norman Island where it was buried. The afore mentioned chest had been secreted away in the cave for 160 years!! A lot of treasure is still unaccounted for.

The famous Scottish author, Robert Louis Stevenson, found out about it and used many of the facts for his story "Treasure Island." You can read all about it in the fascinating book, "The Virgins' Treasure Isle" by, ahem, Julian Putley.

In the evening dinner specials include Baby Back Ribs, cooked just how you like them. There's shrimp curry with Creole or lemon and ginger sauce. Catch of the day is available as is fresh lobster with butter and lemon sauce. Favorites at lunchtime include West Indian Roti, Lobster Salad and an array of burgers.

After dinner the party often goes on into the wee hours with dancing under the stars.

Specialty Drink

Bushwhacker

Ingredients: 2 oz Coco Lopez

2 oz Kahlua

1 oz Vodka

1 oz Creme de Cacao

1 oz Amaretto

2 oz Baileys

Method   Blend with Ice

Serve and sprinkle with nutmeg

Specialty Dishes

Roti

The West Indian Roti is a favorite here. It's a mild curry with potato, chick peas and chicken, fish, goat or beef. The curry is wrapped in an Indian chapati style flat bread and served with mango chutney. Yumm

Pirates Bight
at Norman Island

Pirates Bight

Pirates Bight

It's on the island called Norman
It's casual, you won't find a door man
People did frown
When a fire burned it down
Now, it's back and it's certainly stormin'

Norman's a pirate isle
They like to live in hi-style
It's been a pleasure
To spend all our treasure
Grub'n grog's the best by a mile

Charlie has been a sailing instructor in the BVI for many years. He puts a lot of emphasis on 'rules of the road' and making sure that each and every student is fully aware of his obligations. "If you are the 'stand on' boat you must maintain course and speed," he explains tirelessly. "Only at the very last moment can you deviate from this rule if a collision is imminent."

Now look at this scenario: A catamaran is approaching you on starboard tack. All its fenders are down and the swim ladder is trailing in the water. The mains'l is all the way up on the luff but the second reef is tied in on the clew: the boom is diagonal and pointing at the sky, the sail is a bagged out mess. The genoa is all the way out but not trimmed and the top is luffing wildly, a line trails in the water. While the yacht is making about two knots, the crew is swilling beer and loud rock music can be heard. No doubt they're having fun and no doubt they haven't a clue about sailing. Charlie is on starboard tack too, sailing towards the party boat on a collision course. He's to leeward and the stand on vessel. Someone on the party boat screams across the water "STARBOARD!" unaware that Charlie is the privileged vessel. Charlie immediately bears away to avoid a situation and in so doing he contradicts the rule: 'maintain course and speed.'

In revisiting the situation with his students that night Charlie explained that 'God protects fools and drunks.' For the rest of the week Charlie was referred to as God.

Some charter companies, it seems, regard a good credit card as a suitable sailing qualification in order to allow someone to rent a half million dollar yacht, since more and more incompetence on the water is witnessed every year. In fairness to charter companies it's hard to verify everyone's sailing resume and a few inadequate sailors sometimes slip through the cracks endangering themselves and others.

Now Charlie has a new rule: "Scrutinize the boat you are approaching well in advance. Regardless of who is 'stand on' or 'give way' if the situation merits it, keep clear. It's called the SAFDAF (Stay away from drunks and fools) rule and is likely to be included in the revised edition of the BVI's 'Maritime Charter Yacht Rules and Regulations.'

Pirates by Long Johnsson

Well, now we know it for sure. The pirates of the world are those inhabiting first world industrialized countries while fun loving adventurers in the Caribbean have been taken for a ride. It has become clear that politicians, financiers, captains of industry and corporate executives have been enriching themselves at the expense of all of us. And they were so cunning, quiet and secretive that not an 'Aaaarhhh' could be heard amongst any of 'em. And a lot of struggling 'thought-they-were-pirates' in the Caribbean are not happy about it. In fact they're even planning subtle ways to get revenge.

One pretty young yacht chef Charlie spoke to recently is substituting Whiskas for expensive French pate. "Sour milk sprinkled with ammonia is almost identical to Camembert," she confided. "And there's a certain part of a donkey's anatomy that can double as smoked sausage. We're going to save a fortune.

"Our cuisine is described as Asian/Continental so we'll be offering 'Seafood Bisque.' This is so easy: you just scrape the bottom of the dinghy and the barnacles and seaweed boiled together make a fantastic soup. Sea slugs are everywhere and sliced thin and dressed up with a bit of dildo cactus they make a fine entrée: this specialty I have christened 'Aphrodisiac Gourmand.' It's all in the presentation – and if they don't like it I'll show 'em up in front of all their friends. Anyway, they're usually afraid to admit it for fear of being thought ignorant."

The young lass would've fit right on the Black Pearl, Charlie thought to himself. Next it was the captain's turn to describe his cost cutting ideas and Charlie thought he knew straight away what his answer might be. But he was surprised. Instead of watering down the booze he said he'd decided to charge it up a bit. "Yep, hundred per cent alcohol. Get 'em loaded in a hurry and next morning they won't care where they are. I'll just leave the anchorage, cruise for ten minutes and anchor back in the same spot...oh a few yards away I suppose. Gonna save a fortune in gas. The use of my expensive water toys will be limited to two minutes a day but healthy hiking tours will be encouraged. I mean this is the era of the eco-vacation – gas guzzling water sports are out and heart-healthy hiking is in – and forget what it says on the brochure.

"Snorkeling will be encouraged too; it's relatively eco friendly and cheap. But if they start stepping on fragile brain coral or kicking the spindly and jagged stag horn coral I'll be on 'em in a flash. I just can't afford to let my precious Italian fins get damaged." Charlie nodded sagely. It was going to be a difficult season but Caribbean crews were gearing up for battle.

Bamboushay

Lunch Restaurant in the heart of Road Town
Weekend Party Venue –
  Thursday, Friday Nights

Open Monday thru Friday for Lunch
Live Music on Fridays Nights.

Tel: 342 0303

Free Giveaway
Any Well Drink
(2 for 1)

Bamboushay is the name of a Caribbean dance and this lounge bar has it all happening. Their motto is 'Be Different, Be Unconventional, Be Bamboushay' This cozy little bar/eatery has become the new hotspot for party-goers at week-ends.

    During the week the Bamboushay serves up drinks and lunch and is often used as a place to relax after shopping in the Bamboushay Gallery just behind the restaurant. Their unique pottery, jewelry and island creations will peak the interest of even the most world-weary shopper.

Cryptic Comment

This year I celebrated Thanksgiving in an old-fashioned way. I invited everyone in my neighborhood to my house, we had an enormous feast, and then I killed them and took their land.

Specialty Drink

Climb the Mango Tree

Ingredients: 1 shot Vodka
Mango, Passion and Guava Juices
Soda Water

Method: Stir all ingredients together and pour over ice.
Garnish with a cherry

Specialty Dish

Coconut Curried Chicken

Ingredients: Chunks of thigh meat from chicken. Chicken Stock or Broth
Chopped Onion, diced. Minced Garlic
Grated Ginger, Garam Masala
Curry Powder
Cumin, Coconut Milk
Salt, Pepper

Method: Saute the onions and garlic. Add the chicken and spices and
simmer in chicken broth for about 40 minutes until well
reduced. Finish with coconut milk and season to taste.
Serve with seasoned rice and mango chutney.

Cryptic Comment

**I don't find it hard to
meet expenses, they're everywhere**

Bamboushay

Bamboushay

It's a small night spot in town
Go there, dress up, be a clown
Have a dance if you like
Or a prance with the mic
Live it up, and really 'get down'

Perhaps you're hungry for lunch
Want a snack or something to munch
The Bamboushay
Is the place to stay
You'll be happy here, I have a hunch

Cryptic Comment

I used to think I was
indecisive but now I'm not too sure

BananaKeet Café

Trip Advisor:
Certificate of Excellence. 2013

Superb Location. Best Sunsets in the BVI
Complimentary Sundowner
Local Legend Ruben Chinnery plays
  some Nights
Seating on the Pool Deck
Reservations Strongly Recommended.

Star Giveaway
Bottle of Wine
with Dinner
(Table of four)

Tel: 494-5842 • E mail: info@heritageinnbvi.com
Web Site www.heritageinnbvi.com

The BananaKeet Café is at the Heritage Inn; one of Tortola's most popular Happy Hour bars and restaurants. It is situated on Tortola's north side just above Carrot Bay and only minutes away from Cane Garden Bay.

The dining area is organized around the pool and offers an amazing panoramic view with unforgettable sunsets. On some nights (check for details) the legendary Ruben Chinnery entertains with his 12 string guitar and deep baritone voice. His inventory of songs is extraordinary. Hors d'oeuvres at happy hour include coconut shrimp, wraps, chips and dips, chicken wings and more

The Heritage Inn has nine comfortable rooms each with its own spectacular view and at very reasonable prices. This is a 'must stop' spot!

Cryptic Comment

The Big BANG theory:
God spoke and BANG, it happened

Specialty Drinks

Bananakeet

Ingredients:
- 1 shot Bailey's Irish Cream
- 1 shot Vodka
- Coco Lope
- 1 fresh banana

Method:
Mix all ingredients in a blender with crushed ice.
Finish with grated nutmeg

Passion Smoothie

Ingredients:
- 1 shot amber rum
- 1 shot coconut rum
- 1 shot Triple Sec
- Passion Fruit Juice
- Coco Lopez

Method:
Mix all ingredients in a blender with crushed ice.
Serve over ice cubes.

Specialty Dish

Jerk Pork Loin

Ingredients:
12.5 lb Pork Loin.
Jerk Rub: 1 Tbs Black pepper, 1 Tsp Kocher salt, 1 Tbs Sugar,
1Tbs Ground Ginger (fresh), 1Tbs Ground pimento pepper,
1Tbs Cayenne, 1Tbs Chopped garlic (fresh), ¼ Cup ketchup

Combine all Rub ingredients together and rub entire loin with jerk mixture. Scar loin on hot grill or seal in very hot pan. Place in pre-heated hot oven for about 20 minutes. Rest for five minutes, slice and serve with a good mango chutney.

BananaKeet Café

BananaKeet Café

The name is BananaKeet
You'll find it, give it a Tweet
It's also a bird
No, that's not absurd
But the café is quite a treat

They have the best view on the isle
Not just, but best by a mile
Order up a cold one
Drink under the sun
Make it rum, it's Caribbean style.

| Cryptic Comment |

Women are now against marriage, why? Because women realize it's not worth buying an entire pig, just to get a little sausage.

Brandywine Restaurant

**High End Restaurant. Great Ambiance
Right at the Top of the 'Most Popular'
  in the BVI
Attractive Patio for Hors d'oeuvres, Cocktails**

*Free Giveaway
2 for 1 Mojito*

**Impeccable Service, Mediterranean Menu
Lunch and Dinner Daily, except Tuesday. Reservations Please!
Tel: 495-2301 • www.brandywinerestaurant.com**

Brandywine Restaurant is the longest established fine dining restaurant in the BVI. The emphasis on their menu is largely French with other Mediterranean influences. The restaurant is located ten minutes from Road Town or by boat, a short walk from the bay, and is perched on a hilltop providing panoramic views of the Sir Francis Drake Channel ensuring a cool breeze. The garden style restaurant exudes a warm and intimate atmosphere with art and paintings surrounding the dining areas.

On Friday nights they offer Amuse Bouches with Champagne: tasty hors d'oeuvre bites created from the imagination of chef, Regis.

The lunch menu has such mouth-watering offerings as Salade Nicoise, Chevre Chaud, Sea Bass, Lamb Kebab, Moules Frites, and a selection of Quiches.

For dinner some of your choices are Sea Bass, Salmon, Rack of Lamb, Filet Mignon, Duck Breast and their signature dish, Spanish Paella. For a look at the complete menu access their web site.

The Sunday lunch menu of Roast Beef, Lamb or Pork with Yorkshire Pudding is an island favorite.

Part owner, hostess, Claudine will welcome you with a friendly and personal greeting. The service at Brandywine is renowned.

Note: This little used bay is usually quiet and comfortable for overnight. If the wind goes south of south-east it may be a bit rolly for monohulls but cats will be fine. There is a controlling depth of 10-ft between the reefs at the bay's entrance. Dinghy ashore to the small dock just to the right of the apartments and walk up to the Brandywine Restaurant.

Specialty Drink

Watermelon Mojito

Ingredients:
    Fresh watermelon slice
    Fresh mint
    Freshly squeezed lime juice
    1 shot of white rum

Method:
    Blend the water melon and mint together in a blender, strain and pour over ice with the rum, add the lime juice and serve with a slice of lime and a sprig of mint for garnish

Specialty Dish

Moules Poulette. (Serves 4)

Ingredients:
    4 lbs Fresh PEI mussels
    2 cups of white wine
    2 cups of heavy cream
    1 cup of chopped onion
    1/3 cup of chopped parsley
    2 tsp of chopped garlic
    1 tsp black pepper.
    Roux

Method:
    Put all the above ingredients into a large sauce pan, on full heat and cover until the mussels open. Then remove the mussels from the liquor, reduce and thicken the sauce with a roux. Then add the mussels back into the sauce. Serve with warm French bread and/or French fries

Brandywine Restaurant

Brandywine Restaurant

Brandywine is the place to dine
Pair your meal with a glass of fine wine
The menu has flair
Enjoy Moules Mariniere
Your day will end quite sublime

It's the place for a special occasion
Or perhaps a secret liaison
Follow the sign
To the Brandywine
Go early, avoid the invasion

Cryptic Comment

**The ultimate statistic:
10 out of 10 people die**

Captain Mulligan's

Free Giveaway 2 for 1 Round of Golf

New!! Mini Golf. $10 Per Round
Huge Selection of Pizzas, Build your Own
Giant Screens for Sporting Events

Kids' Parties a Specialty
Giant Dogs, Burgers and More
Free Wi Fi

Tel: 494-0602. • E mail: captainmulligans@gmail.com
www.captainmulligans.com
Reservations please for large groups, 6 persons or more

Captain Mulligan's has evolved into Tortola's premier sports bar and family recreation centre. The fun bar and restaurant specializes in showing all major sporting events live. These include 6 Nations Rugby, all major soccer events, international sailing, NBA Basketball, NHL Hockey and cricket. During these events 'bucket of beer' specials are offered as well as their famous pizzas, burgers and hot dogs.

Mulligan's now offers a mini golf course, a 45 minute a round, 9 hole fun event. This is particularly popular at party time when kids' parties, birthdays and Christmas bashes are organized by both locals and visitors alike. For a fun time make it a Mulligan time!

There's lots of parking, a gift shop with a great selection of Ts. There's free Wi Fi too.

Cryptic Comment

If ignorance is bliss, then tourists are in a constant state of euphoria.

Specialty Drink

Captain's Rum Punch

Method: A unique blend of finest rums combined with Caribbean fruit juices and served over ice. The cocktail is poured over ice cubes and garnished with 'drunken' cherries and freshly grated nutmeg.

Specialty Dish

Mulligan's Pizza

Ingredients and method: A 12" crust is spread with tomato sauce. The pizza is then layered with seasoned ground beef, Italian garlic sausage, red and green bell peppers and slices of pineapple. The pizza is then topped with a generous sprinkling of mozzarella cheese. Yumm!

Cryptic Comment

No matter where you go, you're there. And we're all here because we're not all there!

Captain Mulligan's

Captain Mulligan's

Mulligan is the name in the game
Where a shot can be played again
It's a kind of dance
Where a second chance
Will improve your score and your name

Mulligan's is a sports bar too
With giant TVs for the crew
Then you will know
After watching the show
If they lost, won or just drew

Their burgers are some of the best
Hot dogs as well, no jest
With a cold beer
Give a loud cheer
Cos your team just bettered the rest.

Cryptic Comment

**Nobody's perfect...
I'm a nobody!**

Plumbing

Charlie has been living, eating and sleeping boats for decades and sometimes it's difficult for him to remember that charter guests from places like Missouri, Oklahoma and North Dakota have a hard time comprehending the dynamics pertaining to boats. On one occasion he was explaining the plumbing in the shower and head and one lady was being particularly difficult. "Why doesn't the shower water just drain out like at home?" she asked irritably. Charlie explained patiently that water would come into the boat if there was a drain hole.

The head operation was another point of contention, "Well," she said with a huff, "I'm not putting waste toilet paper in a bin. It'll stink."

"It shouldn't be a problem," explained Charlie. "To prevent blockages you're only allowed one square of paper. And don't forget to put the little lever over to the right when you've finished using the toilet, otherwise the bowl will fill with water and flood the boat when we heel over." Next Charlie demonstrated pumping the head fifteen times and as usual an obnoxious odour filled the cubicle.

"How disgusting," ranted the same woman. "It smells like a sewage works."

"It is a sewage works," said Charlie with a smile. "Well done."

Charlie then went on to explain that conservation of water was a priority and to refill tanks would cost money. More moans and groans - now poor George, the husband, was getting blamed for renting such a primitive boat.

A couple of days into the cruise Charlie heard an exclamation from the guest cabin and it was discovered that some green phosphorescence had found its way into the toilet bowl. Charlie explained.

"This is outrageous," exclaimed the woman. "You mean the toilet is flushed with sea water! That is certainly not hygienic. I shall be complaining to the health authorities when we return."

Charlie was non-plussed. He thought he had explained the plumbing procedures properly. He shook his head in disbelief. Then a smile slowly spread across his face.

Next morning he went snorkeling and as luck would have it he found what he was looking for: a small octopus. He managed to coax it into a plastic baggie and swam with it back to the boat. Later in the day an opportune moment presented itself and he popped it into the guest cabin toilet and closed the lid.

Charlie's plan worked: he knew from the resulting screams that the lady in question had discovered the mini-monster. Next time Charlie vowed he'd find a moray eel and hope that it found a new home!

Cryptic Comment

An old friend explained to Charlie how he could improve his memory, 'Well you see, Charlie, it's like this . . . A herd of buffalo can only move as fast as the slowest buffalo. And when the herd is hunted, it is the slowest and weakest ones at the back that are killed first. This natural selection is good for the herd as a whole, because the general speed and health of the whole group keeps improving by the regular killing of the weakest members. In much the same way, the human brain can only operate as fast as the slowest brain cells. Now, as we know, excessive intake of alcohol kills brain cells. But naturally, it attacks the slowest and weakest brain cells first. In this way, regular consumption of beer eliminates the weaker brain cells, making the brain a faster and more efficient machine. And that, Charlie, is why you always feel smarter after a few beers.'

CruZin

Free Margarita
(2 for 1)

Great West Indian Bar & Grill
Breezy Carrot Bay Location
Grilled Lobster and Seafood Specials
Giant Caribbean Patties:
  Lobster, Conch, Salt Fish and Beef

Cell: 340-3566 • E mail: mariontyre@gmail.com

Cruzin is a bar and grill smack dab in the middle of the pretty village of Carrot Bay. It's just across from the fishermen's wharf where the fresh fish and lobster are landed daily. Owner/operator Lena Penn has spent years honing her cooking skills on charter yachts. She grew up in Carrot Bay and the restaurant's beautiful location has been in the family for decades. Al fresco dining is provided with shade being offered by a huge Mother -in-law's Tongue tree. The strange name comes from the continuous noise the tree makes when even the gentlest of breezes is blowing. (Sorry Ma).

Cruzin has a truly Caribbean ambiance with a menu to prove it. Apart from their famous patties they serve curried mutton, fresh fish, shrimp and lobster. The CruZin kitchen makes homemade Jack Daniels bbq sauce for their sumptuous ribs and a Chicken Marsala. All dishes may be spiced up with Lena's homemade hot sauce.

This Caribbean hideaway is also famous for its fresh fruit smoothies: Papaya, Guava, Soursap, Mango and Banana. All the fruits are locally grown.

New owner Mac is dedicated to making Cruzin a 'must stop' spot. He knows and loves the BVI and has been residing here, on and off, for over twenty years. Sushi and sashimi are often featured on the menu.

Specialty Drink

Captain Charley

Ingredients: 1 shot Midori (melon liqueur)
1 shot Coconut Rum
2 oz Cranberry Juice
2 oz Pineapple Juice.

Method: Mix together all ingredients and pour over ice.
Shout 'Cheers Buccaneers' before enjoying your first swallow.

Specialty Dish

Swahili Wings

Cruzin's Swahili Wings have a spicy Asian flair. The wings are tossed in a spicy blend, cooked in the oven (not battered or fried) and served their secret sauce.

Cryptic Comment

Beer is the greatest invention of mankind. The wheel was also a great invention but it doesn't go so well with pizza

CruZin

CruZin

Carrot Bay is the place to be
The breeze comes right off the sea
Then a CruZin dish
Of Carrot Bay fish
Is the best, just believe me

Have a Cruzin smoothie with rum
After playin' all day in the sun
Undo the last zip
'n take a quick dip
Be a mermaid, it's all about fun!

Cryptic Comment

Met a beautiful girl down at the park today. Sparks flew, she fell at my feet and we ended up having sex there and then. God, I love my new Taser!

D' Best Cup

Great Location near Village Cay Marina, Road Town
The Best Assorted Coffees in Town
Specializing in Breakfasts and Lunches.
Large Selection of Salads and Sandwiches

Free Giveaway 2 free regular coffees with 2 sandwiches

Free Wi Fi
Breakfast: 7.30 to 11am. Lunch 11am to 3-00pm

Tel: 494-0194

D' Best Cup is a well established coffee shop. The coffee used is a secret and provides all the many items on the menu with their unique flavor.

The emphasis on their food menu is sandwiches - made with French baguettes or multi-grain bread.

Their breakfast special is a sandwich with scrambled egg, a choice of bacon, sausage, turkey or ham with cheese optional. BLTs and Club Sandwiches are also available.

A large variety of sandwiches is available for lunch and salads are also on the menu: Garden, Caesar or Chicken Caesar.

A popular branch of D' Best Cup is located at Soper's Hole, West End.

Cryptic Comment

A day without sunshine is like.....night?

Specialty Drink

Specialty Coffees

D' Best Cup serves up Flavored Lattes, Espresso, Cappuccino, Mocha , Macchiato as well as regular American style coffee, hot or iced. Various Teas and Hot Chocolate are also available. Other drinks include Smoothies, Milk Shakes, Italian Sodas and Cremosas.

Specialty Dish

Pan-seared Steak Baguette

A portion of steak is seasoned and pan seared while a mini baguette is toasted. The steak is sliced, layered onto the baguette and topped with a spiced Asian dressing. The sandwich is served with lettuce, tomato and a julienne of pickled carrots flavored with coriander. Yumm!

Cryptic Comment

**They say that sex is
the best form of exercise.
Now correct me if I'm wrong but I don't think
2 minutes and 15 seconds every 6 months is
going to shift this beer belly**

D' Best Cup

D' Best Cup

It's right in the heart of town
Have it white, black or just brown
Perhaps an Espresso
You poor old fellow
It'll bring you right up if you're down

Order a sandwich of turkey
Or a breakfast, a toasted BLT
Whether for lunch
I have a hunch
You'll be back again, just you see

Cryptic Comment

A Muslim was sitting
next to Paddy on a plane. Paddy ordered a
whiskey. The stewardess asked the Muslim if
he'd like a drink.
He replied in disgust "I'd rather be raped by a
dozen whores than let liquor touch my lips!"
Paddy handed his drink back and said,
"Me too, I didn't know we had a choice!"

The Dove

RESTAURANT & WINE BAR

Tortola's Best Restaurant.
 Awards 2011 2012 2013
Warm Ambiance.
 Professional Friendly Staff
Wine Spectator Award of Excellence 2013
New Gelateria and Coffee Bar

Free Giveaway Glass of their best house wine with dinner

Open 5pm till late. Dinner: 6pm till 10pm
Reservations Highly Recommended

Tel: 494-0313 • www.thedovebvi.com
E mail: dovebvi@hotmail.com

The Dove is a quietly elegant cottage restaurant in the heart of Road Town. The restaurant was converted from a traditional wood-framed West Indian house which creates a warm and cozy ambiance. Now in its eleventh year it is still widely regarded as the best restaurant in the BVI.

Chef Travis Philips has been with the restaurant for about five years and his skills combining both French and Japanese cuisines into a fusion have been much appreciated by customers from around the world.

Chef Travis creates seasonal menus which feature the best ingredients that can be sourced. Every item on the menu is made from scratch in their own kitchen, including our pastas, assorted charcuterie, ice cream and all condiments.

The Dove boasts the largest wine list in the BVI, all stored in a special temperature controlled room. The cocktail menu changes seasonally as well and features the freshest ingredients and newest concepts. Dine in the intimate air-conditioned dining room or come for a cocktail and bar snacks in the open air patio. Reservations highly suggested for dinner.

Specialty Drink

Wine

The Dove prides itself on its award winning wine list. A large selection of wines by the glass

Specialty Dishes

Appetizer - Ahi Tuna

Fresh Ahi Tuna with grapefruit, cucumber, gin & arugula sprouts, black pepper tomato concasse, pine nut puree and cassava chips.

Main - The Dove Steak

This Angus beef rib eye is encrusted with mushrooms and parmesan cheese. It is served with black truffle jus, white truffle oil, blue cheese potato pave, prosciutto wrapped asparagus, and a balsamic reduction.

Cryptic Comment

'OLD' is when your friends compliment you on your new alligator shoes ... and you're barefoot!

The Dove

The Dove

The Dove is the place to dine
And to order a glass of fine wine
If you're in love
Go to the Dove
And sample the fruits of the vine

Perhaps have a plate of fresh fish
It's nothing short of delish
A glass of cool white
Might be your delight
To enhance this favorite dish

Cryptic Comment

Religion has convinced people that there's an invisible man...living in the sky, who watches everything you do every minute of every day. And the invisible man has a list of ten specific things he doesn't want you to do. And if you do any of these things, he will send you to a special place, of burning and fire and smoke and torture and anguish for you to live forever, and suffer and burn and scream until the end of time. But he loves you. He loves you and he needs money.

Emile's Sports Bar and Grill

**Tortola's only Mexicana Cantina
Completely Renovated, Warm Ambiance.
Large TVs in the Bar, Large Pizza Menu.
New Patio Bar with Projector, Big Screen**

**Happy Hour and Dinner
7 Days. 3pm till late.**

Tel: 495-1775

Free Giveaway
Chairman's
Sweet 'n Sour
2 for 1

Emile's is Tortola's only Mexicana Cantina. Located opposite Harbor View Marina in East End this delightful restaurant and sports bar is easily reached by dinghy or vehicle with ample dinghy docking or car parking space. The bar/restaurant has been completely renovated with air conditioning and an attractive patio for diners. There is a casual ambiance and manageress Junie will take care of you while Chef Zach will answer queries and requests.

There is an extensive selection on the bar menu from Stuffed Jalapenos, Chef's Chili, a Nacho Platter and more... Main courses include their 'special' Carnitas, Blackened Mahi and a Vegetarian Napoleon, to name but a few. There is also a large pizza menu.

Caribbean special nights invite you to partake of a Pig Roast on Mondays and on Fridays the ever popular Fish Fry.

Cryptic Comment

**If everything's coming
your way you're in the wrong lane**

Specialty Drink

Chairman's Sweet 'n Sour

Ingredients: 1 shot Chairman's Reserve Rum
Orange Juice
Fresh Squeezed Lime
Simple Syrup

Method: Mix together all ingredients, pour over ice and garnish with a slice of lime

Specialty Dish

Carnitas, Rice and Beans

Ingredients and method: A loin or shoulder of Pork is well seasoned and slowly pot roasted or simmered until tender. The meat is then 'pulled' and served on a flour tortilla with a bean salsa and rice. The dish is topped with sour cream and sprinkled with cilantro. Yumm!

Cryptic Comment

"Thank you for sending me a copy of your book; I'll waste no time reading it"

Emile's Sports Bar and Grill

Emile's Sports Bar and Grill

Ever been to a Mexi Cantina
To find a cute Senorita
You may be in luck
But if you get stuck
Just become a very good eater

Come see the latest football
Emile's is for one and all
It should be seen
On the giant screen
It'll be your very best call

Charlie loves wine. Ever since he got a touch of gout he slowed down on his beer drinking and took to wine. The French and Italians loved him more, the Germans and Brits made fun of him and the Americans were ambivalent. But Charlie never became a wine snob. In restaurants he even overlooked the rather ostentatious habit of tasting a drop before pouring for the table. Then, as he began to order a bottle of wine to accompany a meal out he noticed the prices were somewhat out of proportion. A drinkable bottle in the liquor store was $7.00 but was marked up to $45 on the restaurant's wine list. A rip off, he thought. One night he took his own bottle and was told by a rather timid waitress that a corkage charge of $15 would be applied to his bill. "Corkage!" he said angrily, "It's a screw top."

As time went on Charlie understood wines and their qualities better and better. He knew that a full bodied wine was rounded and flavorful. He understood a white wine that was crisp and dry might well be good company for a heavy fish dish like turbot with a cream sauce or a lobster thermidor. A strong sweet wine might go well with a dessert.

One day Charlie came across a bottle of wine by a little known South African vineyard. The wine in question was 'completely new.' Its name was Femme Facile. The wine was listed in a nautical magazine as being appropriate for clientele that frequented seafood restaurants. As a nautical man it sounded just up Charlie's alley. Then he read the wine taster's expert evaluation: Delicate bouquet of oysters, a nose of fresh mussel, a full bodied flavor of tuna sushi, after taste of essence of clam with a whiff of Indian Ocean current. A single phrase summed it up: A fragrance of karma sutra. It was described as the 'ultimate aphrodisiac' and 'might even save the rhinoceros.' Charlie just had to try some. He invited his favorite girlfriend to dinner at a seafood restaurant and ordered a bottle of Femme Facile. Well, to cut a long story short, she took one sip and immediately spat it into her soup bowl declaring it undrinkable. Charlie, who quite liked it, apologized and ordered her a martini, straight up and then another, and then a third. She was happy and bubbly the whole evening and later on he had his way with her (and she had her way too) .

Sailing with Charlie

Charlie pondered the evening and eventually came to the conclusion that perhaps it was described as an aphrodisiac because it made customers wish for something stronger.

Then, the other day Charlie saw the mega yacht Serena. It's a gleaming multi-million dollar mega yacht with many tiers of decks, helicopter pads, Jacuzzis, swimming pools, bars and restaurants, a submarine and an army of staff to keep the whole thing running smoothly. Charlie found out that the owner made his fortune dealing Stolichnaya vodka: zillions from peddlin' poison.

Charlie is now looking for investors in his new business venture; an international dealership for 'Femme Facile.'

Cryptic Comment

How to achieve inner peace:
I'm passing this on because it worked for me today.
A doctor on TV said in order to have inner peace, we should always finish things we start, & that we all could use more calm in our lives. I looked around my house to find things I'd started but haven't finished...I finished off a bottle of Merlot, a bodle of Vodka, a butle of wum, tha mainder of Valiuminum pscriptions, an a box of chocletz.
Yu haf no idr how fablus I feel right now.
Sned this to all who need inner piss. An telum u luvum...

Fish 'n Lime

fish n' lime inn

**Old Jolly Roger...Completely Renovated
Right on the Water, Dinghy Dock.**

**Specializing in Fresh Fish and Lobster
Happy Hour $2 off Every Drink. Free Wi Fi
Lounge Bar, Satellite TV, Rooms Available**

**Tel: 495-4276 • E Mail: info@fishnlime.com
www. fishnlime.com**

The Fish 'n Lime is the new bar and restaurant at Soper's Hole, West End, Tortola. For those who knew the Jolly Roger Inn, the Fish 'n Lime is the new name and the location has had a complete overhaul. The bar has a new, fresh look with tiled surface and comfy seating. The kitchen has been relocated down to deck level to facilitate more efficient service. Todd, the chef, is an experienced island chef having managed many a kitchen around the islands. Simon, the head bar tender, comes from the much loved Willy T. while Heather is the owner/manager and directs all the operations. The emphasis of the restaurant is fresh fish and fishermen bring their catch straight to the dock every day. Already the restaurant is receiving rave reviews. The location is especially popular with yachties who can dinghy right up to the bar and tie up

There will be special events hosted by the restaurant: sailing events like IC 24 regattas, the Sweethearts Regatta and others. There have already been darts tournaments and live bands and special events will be forthcoming.

Rooms are available for B and B and longer term. These are especially handy for those wishing to catch an early ferry. A lounge bar with satellite TV is also on the premises

Specialty Drink

F'n Lemonade

Ingredients: 1 shot Citrus Vodka
Lemon Juice
Cranberry Juice
Ginger and Peppercorn Syrup
Ginger Ale

Method: Mix all ingredients together except the ginger ale, pour over ice cubes, top off with the bubbly soda. Garnish with a slice of lemon. Refreshing!

Specialty Dish

Fresh Fish

The Fish 'n Lime specializes in freshly caught and grilled fish and lobster... with plenty of lime, of course!

fish n' lime inn

Fish 'n Lime

Fish 'n Lime

It's the bar to go for a blast
Pirates 'n yachtsmen, the cast
The babes can be hot
But others are not
Don't worry! You won't be out classed

This place is all about fish
And fish just make the best dish
Baked, boiled or fried
I think I have tried
Every one on my list that's a wish

LE GRAND
Café deux

Le Grand Café

Open for Lunch and Dinner
 (Reservation for Dinner Please)
Dining in a Beautiful Garden Setting
Centrally located on Waterfront Drive,
 Road Town
Late Night Parties Friday and Saturday Nights

Tel: 494-8660. Facebook: Le Grand Cafe

Le Grand Café is situated on Waterfront Drive in Road Town close to the ferry dock. Formerly Le Cabanon this popular restaurant and night spot is back with a bang. Lunches are served daily and can be enjoyed al fresco in a cool garden setting. The Doner Kebab is a popular lunch time dish. Dinner choices include Filet Mignon with a Peppercorn Sauce, Rib Eye Steak and Fresh Fish. Other specialty items include Escargot, Foie Gras and an exotic Cheese Platter. Le Grand Café is now specializing in dishes using the best and freshest foods. "Grilled and smoked dishes are our prioriety," says Manager Paul," We are striving to find the finest unprocessed and natural food. 'Quality at Affordable Prices' is our catch phrase."

Long known for late night revelry Friday night is party night with dancing to a professional DJ. A late night 'happy hour' is also offered to enhance the fun. On Saturdays there's live music, so get on down to Le Grand Café for party action.

Specialty Drink

 Mojito

Ingredients:
- 1 shot white rum
- Simple Syrup
- Juice from a whole lime
- Mint leaves
- Sparkling Water

Method: The lime juice is added to the simple syrup and mint leaves. The mint leaves are bruised to release the essential oils. Then the rum is added and the mixture is briefly stirred to lift the mint leaves up from the bottom for better presentation. The drink is poured over ice cubes and topped with the sparkling soda water. Garnish with mint leaves and a slice of lime.

Specialty Dish

The Doner Kebab

Ingredients and method: Unique to the BVI this wonderful Middle Eastern dish is all the rave on the island. This vertical style barbecue involves layers of lamb or beef slices placed on a barbecue, well spiced and turned until done. The carver slices off portions and serves the meat on flat bread or in a pita pocket with sliced tomato, lettuce and onion.

Cryptic Comment

When I'm drunk my wife hates me. When I'm sober I hate her

LE GRAND

Café deux

Le Grand Café

Le Grand Café

It's party night at Le Grand
Saturday night, and they've got a band
Are you a nun?
No! Go and have fun
Celebrate in festival land

It's the best night spot in town
Put a smile on your face, not a frown
After good food
You'll be in the mood
So get up, then really 'get down'

**I had a rose named after
me and I was very flattered. But I was not
pleased to read the description in the catalog:
"Not good in a bed, but fine against a wall." --
Eleanor Roosevelt**

The Beef Island Guest House
& de Loose Mongoose
Restaurant

The Loose Mongoose

"Get Loose at the Goose"

Beach Bar on the Sand
Breakfast, Lunch and Dinner
Brand New Menu
Spacious, Comfortable Rooms with
Complimentary Continental Breakfast

(Walking Distance to Airport)

Now under new management.

Tel: 495-2303 • E mail: mongoose@surfbvi.com
www.beefislandguesthouse.com

The Loose Mongoose is a delightful beach bar and restaurant. For decades it's been the place to go for good meals at affordable prices. Now, with a new chef, exciting things are happening.

Besides live music on several nights, sports enthusiasts love the two 32" TVs that show all the major sporting events, from the Superbowl, Basketball Championships and the World Series of Baseball. Major sailing events and regattas are also popular. Pig roast on Full Moon Nights, Barbecue and Live Music some Nights.

Yep! There's always something going on at the Loose Mongoose.

Specialty Drink

Melon Colada

Ingredients: 2 shots amber rum
1 shot melon liqueur
1 ounce Coco Lopez

Method: Mix all ingredients and pour over ice or blend with crushed ice.
Garnish with a maraschino cherry.

Specialty Dish

Pig Roast on Full Moon Nights

Cryptic Comment

I heard a guy complaining about how expensive his wedding is going to be. Wait till he finds out how much his divorce will cost!

The Beef Island Guest House
& de Loose Mongoose
Restaurant

The Loose Mongoose

The Loose Mongoose

The location is at Trellis Bay
A most wonderful place to play
They have a guest house
You won't find a mouse
But a mongoose might come to stay

This bar's called the Loose Mongoose
Have a meal and then some fine booze
The wind's from the east
And provides a good breeze
After drinks in the sun, have a snooze

My sex life is like a Ferrari. I don't have a Ferrari

Myett's

Open all Year, Right on the Beach
Breakfast, Brunch, Lunch and Dinner
Happy Hour with Live Entertainers

Star Giveaway Bottle of Wine with Dinner

Wi Fi, Laundry, Gift Shop, ATM
Spa Service and AC Rooms

Tel: 495-9649 • E mail: thebeatgoeson@myetts.com
www.myettent.com • facebook: myetts cane garden bay

Myetts, on the beach at Cane Garden Bay, is a cleverly designed complex that uses natural surroundings, man-made gardens and tropical foliage to provide a truly Caribbean setting. Kareem Rhymer opened in 1992 and with wife Valerie has been expanding and improving the popular beach bar/ restaurant ever since. The location is far enough away from the crowds at the other end of the beach to afford some privacy and there's always a shady spot under the palms for a happy hour drink.

Myett's is open for breakfast, lunch and dinner. 'Fast Breakfasts' are now offered for those on their way to work or other appointments. Every evening there's a theme menu. It might be a Pizza Night, Caribbean Buffet or a Mexican Night. Recently a new Beach Bar has been added with 'toes in the sand' ambiance. There's a 'Bar Eats' menu with very reasonably priced appetizers like Cracked Conch, BBQ Chicken Wings, Nachos, BBQ Ribs and more. Myett's Happy Hour is now famous island wide with talented musicians playing every evening.

Myett's is fully integrated with eco standards and uses no Styrofoam or plastic cups. Cups made from corn by-product are used as well as for their drinking straws. At their property out back a glass blowing facility offers visitors a fascinating glimpse of this clever art. Unique souvenirs are made from recycled bottles – and there are plenty of those in the BVI.

Plans for the future include the services of a concierge/activities director. One trip on the drawing board is a 'Rum Tour' taking in the Callwood's Distillery, Bomba's Shack and Pusser's. Other events are likely to follow so keep your eyes and ears open. There's always something going on at Myett's.

Specialty Drink

Myett's Delight

Ingredients: 1 shot Myett's Rum
Fruit Punch
Splash of Pineapple
Coco Lopez

Method: Blend all ingredients with a cup of crushed ice. Serve in a long glass. Floater of dark rum optional. Top with grated nutmeg and garnish with a cherry.

Specialty Dish

BBQ

Myett's is famous for its barbecued ribs, chicken and fish. They make their own bbq sauce, which is absolutely delicious. The recipe is secret.

Cryptic Comment

**Men DO have feelings.
They often feel hungry!**

Myett's

Myett's

Happy hour here is a blast
Sing with the rest of the cast
You're bound to have fun
Yes! Fun in the sun
Myett's is always a blast

With music there's sure to be dancin'
And pretty girls for all to be glancin'
A gyrating booty
On a dark skin beauty
Will have all the boys up and advancin'

Cryptic Comment

Corduroy pillows:
They're making headlines!

Conch

"We're going to have conch for dinner," exclaimed the very independently-minded tourist pronouncing the word 'contch.' "Look, I've collected a pile over there on the beach."

"OK," said Charlie, apprehensively, "you'll need to clean them, slice them and tenderize them before you cook them." Charlie was not a fan of conch. In his opinion the taste was not enticing, the texture rubbery and the resulting conch fritters (the dish of choice by most tourists) were deep fried balls of dough with bits of conch mixed in. They were designed to stop your heart pumping. The excited 16 year old grabbed a bucket and some tools and headed to the beach. After half an hour Charlie glanced over to the sandy spot where the likely lad was now attempting to smash the conch into submission with a large rock. He was covered in bits of shell, various and sundry conch body parts and gelatinous dribbly bits. He stopped every few seconds to swat the ever increasing swarm of biting insects. Charlie took pity on the hapless youth. He swam over to the beach, showed the intrepid food gatherer how to make a slit in the shell in the right place to cut the muscle to extract the doubtful gastropod and then instructed him how to remove the inedible bits and clean off the jelly that adheres to it like...something sticks to a blanket.

An hour later the youth arrived back at the boat covered in red blotches from insect bites. He was carrying several lumps of slimy, multi-colored meat covered in a combination of sand and mucous, "Mum," he called out, "I've brought dinner." He plunked it down on the counter and said, "Charlie, do you know which the edible sea urchins are? I saw a few over by the rocks. Perhaps we could try some for hors d'oeuvres."

Charlie sighed inwardly but put on a brave face. "The edible ones are the white ones with short spines. There's about a teaspoonful of yellow roe on the inside of the shell. You'll need a bucketful for four people."

"I heard it tastes like caviar. I'll pick up plenty so that you can have the biggest portion."

"Oh, the kid has a heart of gold," thought Charlie with a groan, definitely a dangerous thing in a 16 year old. Another hour passed and then the dinghy approached and our valiant adventurer handed Charlie the bucket. It contained some orange substance floating in a mixture of dirty water, shell fragments and brownish shellfish intestines. Charlie had seen vomit look more appetizing. "Nice score," he said to the smiling lad.

At 6pm Charlie announced to the family that he was going ashore to visit friends. "Don't wait up," he shouted as he sped away in the dinghy. It was much later when he returned after several libations. He entered the dimly lit main salon and found a plate of food waiting for him. There was even a half bottle of white wine sitting next to his plate. Although he was hungry he quietly went on deck and scraped the food over the side.

In the morning Mum asked, "How did you enjoy the coconut shrimp in curry sauce?"

Charlie blinked for a moment, "Delicious," he lied. "What happened to the conch?"

"Over the side," whispered Mum conspiratorially. "You didn't think we'd eat that did you?"

Peg Legs

Restaurant (Lunch and Dinner),
Beach Bar on the Water
(7 days, open late)
"Best Happy Hour on Tortola" 5-7pm daily
Friday Happy Hour – Free Pizza at the Beach Bar

Star Giveaway
Bottle of Wine
with Dinner

Reservations Strongly Recommended

Tel: 494-0028 • www.nannycay.com

Peg Legs at Nanny Cay has continuously evolved to become one of the most attractive locations in the BVI. The beach bar between the pool and the restaurant is a popular watering hole just off the beach. Every day between 5 and 7pm is happy hour and on Friday free pizza is passed around for all to enjoy. The restaurant, now under NEW management is becoming an island favorite. The extensive menu is reasonably priced with most entrees well under $30. There's even a fresh vegetable risotto for health conscious customers. Lunch can be eaten al fresco on the beach under shade palapas and the beach bar is right there for your convenience. A pizza menu is available with many enticing options and a 'lighter fare' menu may well be just the ticket for the kids. For those with a good appetite the 'Big Peg Leg Burger' will probably fit the bill: A 10oz Angus ground sirloin burger with fried onions, bacon, pineapple, lettuce, tomato, cheese and pickle. Jimmy Buffett; eat your heart out!

Nanny Cay has become the premier destination for BIG events. Nanny Cay hosts the hugely popular BVI Spring Regatta, the Charter Boat Show, Halloween Party, Gaming Night (proceeds to the Animal Shelter) and the Caribbean 1500 Rally, to name but a few.

Nanny Cay' Peg Legs is a fun destination and one not to be missed by visitors and yachtsmen alike.

Specialty Drink

Two Rum Punch

Ingredients: 1 shot Cruzan Gold
                       Tropical fruit juices.
                       Floater of Myer's dark rum

Method: Pour ingredients over ice and garnish with a cherry.

Specialty Dish

Pork Loin

Ingredients: The pork is seasoned well with herbs and spices. Then it is pan seared, finished slowly and served with a cream sauce laced with port. The dish is presented with vegetables and sides of your choice.

Cryptic Comment

They begin the evening news with 'Good Evening,' then proceed to tell you why it isn't.

Peg Legs

Peg Legs

In a battle I lost a good leg
So now I walk with a peg
It don't stop me drinkin'
With glasses a clinkin'
I'll drink it to the last dreg

The bar tender, she's such a dear
"Serve me up a glass of cold beer"
She's a real tease
So I'll give her a squeeze
My intentions will then be quite clear

Cryptic Comment

I've just watched a
documentary about children being beaten and
abused in Indian sweat shops. Looking at the
quality of stitching on my new trainers the little
bastards deserved it!

Quito's Gazebo

Tortola's Hottest Nightspot
Quito and his Band The Edge Fridays
Quito solo most other nights
Intimate atmosphere. World Class Reggae
Lunch and Dinner served daily

Free Giveaway, Quito's Legend (2 for1)

Tel: 495-4837 • VHF: CH 16 • www.quitorymer.com

Since the mid 80s Quito's has been the hottest nightspot in Tortola. Native son Quito Rhymer is a talented artist and musician as well as a successful businessman and most nights the club is thronging with a diverse group of partygoers and music fans. The Gazebo is right on the beach at beautiful Cane Garden Bay with a spectacular view over the water to Jost van Dyke. The stage is set back behind a small dance floor and on Friday and Saturday nights, giant speakers pump out the live reggae rhythms of Quito and his popular band "The Edge." On most other nights Quito will play solo in a somewhat more intimate atmosphere. In the early evening the restaurant on the veranda serves island style food with the emphasis on fish dishes.

Over the years Quito has become very popular locally and a plethora of CDs are testament to his skill as an imaginative and prolific entertainer. You can catch the real Caribbean island flavor here.

Quito's Legend

Ingredients:
- 1 shot white Bacardi rum
- 1 shot Smirnoff vodka
- 1 shot peach schnapps
- 1 shot blue Curacao
- 1 ounce sweet and sour (sugar syrup and lime)
- 3 ounces 7-Up
- 1 ounce grenadine

Method: Pour into a 12 ounce glass over ice cubes the rum, vodka and peach schnapps. Slowly add blue Curacao and syrup. Carefully add the 7up and slowly pour in the grenadine. The final cocktail should have a layered look: orange, blue and pink. Garnish with an orange slice, lime slice and a maraschino cherry.

Cryptic Comment

**Due to a water shortage
the municipal swimming baths in Dublin are
closing lanes 7 and 8**

Quito's Gazebo

Quito's Gazebo

Visit Quito's, it's always a blast
The reggae's a blast from the past
It's time for a party
With look-alike Marley
Bob's in the superstar class

The 'Edge' is the name of the band
The best reggae band in the land
Rasta's they love it
Tourists aren't above it
Dance on the beach in the sand

So if you're feeling sad and alone
Get a taxi to Quito's from home
Or give him a call
Come on down, have a ball
Unless you're 'hotter on the phone'

Cryptic Comment

Change is inevitable, except from a vending machine

Rhymer's Beach Bar

Rhymer's Beach Bar

**Right on the beach, Deck chairs,
Shade umbrellas
Gift shop, Beauty salon, Laundromat
Ice and Grocery shop
Breakfast, Lunch and Dinner**

**Tel: 495-4639 • Cell: 542-6064 • E mail: rhymers@surfbvi.com
www.canegardenbaybeachhotel.com**

"We look after you!"

Rhymers was one of the first hotels on Cane Garden Bay and it continues to be popular today.

Proprietress Patsy Rhymer provides single, double and family rooms and details can be accessed on the quoted web site

Cane Garden Bay is one of Tortola's finest beaches with calm, clear water and magnificent views. This is a place not to miss.

Specialty Drink

Bushwhacker

Ingredients:
- 1 shot vodka
- 1 shot Khalua
- 1 shot Tia Maria
- 1 shot Baileys
- 2 T spoons Coco Lopez

Method: Blend all ingredients with ice and serve in chilled glass

Specialty Dish

Conch Fritters

Ingredients:
- Chopped and tenderized conch
- Finely diced onions, red and green sweet peppers
- Secret spices
- Beer batter

Method: Combine all ingredients and spoon into balls.
Deep fry in hot oil and serve with Hollandaise sauce

Rhymer's Beach Bar

Rhymer's Beach Bar

Rhymer's is right on the beach
Have a conch fritter, one each
You'll be glad that you did
And so will your kid
Cos conch is better than plonk

Dine with a glass of chilled wine
Cos to dine without wine is a crime
The wine will enhance
The evening, then dance
Under the stars, it's sublime

Cryptic Comment

**When a lady is pregnant,
all her friends touch the stomach and say "congrats." But none of them come and touch the man's penis and say "good job."
Sexism is alive and well!**

Sailor's Rest

Charming location at Black Point
next to Quito's, Cane Garden Bay
Open for breakfast, lunch and dinner

Wide selection of local, seafood & continental dishes

Tel: 495-9908 • VHF Ch 16 • E mail: bvilighthouse@surfbvi.com
www.travel-watch.com/lighthouse

The Sailors' Rest is located at the end of the dinghy dock in Cane Garden Bay. It is nestled into the hillside in a most artistic way with a bubbling fountain and nooks and crannies providing seating in several different settings. The main location features the bar which has a delightful view looking along the sweeping panorama of Cane Garden Bay Beach and out over the sea to Jost van Dyke. The menu includes many varieties of burgers for lunch; fresh fish and local specialties like octopus, sword fish, coconut shrimp and mahi mahi for dinner.

Everywhere you look there are hints of artistry and history. The BVI has a strong nautical heritage and proprietress Malcia Rymer has used her personal memories to enhance the décor of her restaurant. There are models of the many inter-island sailing craft that would ply the local waters. Their owners and captains are memorialized in a framed plaque and interesting photographs of bygone days add to the charming ambiance of this new Cane Garden Bay attraction.

The Sailors' Rest is also offering its unique venue for wedding receptions, renewal of vows, birthday parties, anniversaries, baby and bridal showers. If attendees become too numerous then people can spill over into Quito's Gazebo, after all Malcia is Quito's sister. Another advantage to this location for those 'special events' is that Ms Rymer is the owner/operator of the Lighthouse Hotel with self-catering rooms and apartments for couples and families. So you can stay over for the night, weekend or week. See the website for details.

Specialty Drink

The Constellation

Ingredients:
- 1 shot Baileys
- 1 shot brandy
- 1 shot Amaretto
- 1 shot Kahlua
- 1 ounce Coco Lopez

Method:
- Mix in blender with ice until creamy.
- Pour over ice and garnish with a cherry and slice of orange

Specialty Dish

Coconut Curried Lobster

Ingredients:
- Curry powder
- Tomato paste
- Chopped Onions
- Chopped red and green peppers
- Freshly minced garlic, salt and pepper
- Coconut milk
- Par cooked lobster chunks

Method:
- Shallow fry the finely chopped onions and peppers.
- Add the garlic, tomato paste, coconut milk and curry powder.
- A cup of water may be added if necessary.
- Simmer for 10 minutes, add the lobster chunks and cook for a further five minutes. Season to taste.
- Serve with Caribbean rice and fresh vegetables of the day

Sailor's Rest

Sailor's Rest

The Sailors' Rest
Is one of the best
In the whole of Cane Garden Bay
It's the cutest bar
The newest star
That's what most people say

You'll see it first
So quench your thirst
At the bar called the Sailors' Rest
A bight to eat
Is hard to beat
You're sure to love it, no jest.

Cryptic Comment

"Just booked a table for me and the wife for Valentine's Day. I hope it doesn't end in tears – she's hopeless at snooker"

Sailing with Charlie

Floggings and other Fun Punishments

'The Beatings will continue until Morale Improves' is the single most popular banner on T shirts bought by tourists in the BVI. The irony is lost on no-one. But it was not long ago that flogging was an accepted and effective form of punishment meted out to school boys, mariners, law breakers and criminals. Charlie can remember his own purple, blue and black buttocks from schooldays a mere thirty years ago.

In the British navy the cruel and barbaric punishment of flogging was inflicted for relatively minor crimes, like stealing an extra weevil at lunch. And 'six of the best' (the schoolboys' beating) was pretty tame compared to a flogging with a cat o' nine tails. Floggings were meted out to those found guilty of thieving, disobedience and mutiny. For striking an officer a 'flogging around the fleet' was often the punishment with lashes given at the gangway of every ship. Few survived a severe flogging.

A slice of bread stolen from a bakery would mean transportation to the penal colony of Australia; a voyage of months with no prospects at the end.

At the other extreme during the 18th century several mundane crimes were punishable by execution. The 'Bloody Code,' as the regimen was known, was responsible for executing offenders for: 'scrumping' (stealing apples from trees in a private orchard), use of obscene language, the cutting down of a tree, stealing a rabbit from a warren, being out and about with a blackened face (definitely worrisome for West Indian crew), poaching and damaging Westminster Bridge.

Charlie has found the recent historical revelations to be most helpful on his charters. He has made a list of offences and punishments and pinned them up on a conspicuous bulkhead.

1. Blocked head: six lashes

2. Being sea sick over the windward rail: ten lashes

3. Not allowing nubile young daughter to go ashore for drinks with captain: transportation to Australia

4. Whingeing about the weather: six lashes

5. Not leaving adequate tip: summary execution

6. Having hellacious hangover: forgiveness (occupational hazard)

7. Asking dumb questions: six lashes

8. Asking same dumb questions again: ten lashes

9. Not stowing items properly: six lashes

10. Leaving hatches or ports open while underway: transportation to anywhere miles from the sea

11. Whingeing about anything: six lashes

12. Not being ecstatic about the best sailing vacation in the world: the beatings shall continue until morale improves

Hey, lubbers have to learn, and who am I to refute the rulings of our wise elders of yore?

Cryptic Comment

**Just changed my
Facebook name to No-One.
So when someone posts a stupid comment I
can click 'No-One likes this.'**

Scaramouche

Late night club atmosphere with music and dancing till late

An Upstairs and Downstairs at
  Breezy Soper's Hole
Delicious Italian Menu, Bar Lounge with
  Ambiance
Italian Aperitivo Menu, Italian Coffees
Breakfast, Lunch and Dinner and Post Dinner Lounge Drinks.
Reservations Please! Open 6am to 2am

Free Orange Passion (2 for1)

Tel: 343-1602 • E mail: info@scaramouchebvi.com
www.scaramouchebvi.com

Scaramouche is an Italian restaurant with a difference. The accent is on casual elegance with style. There are two levels: a downstairs for breakfast, coffees, casual lunches and aperitivos. The Italian ambiance is enhanced by easy listening music, comfy furniture and soft lighting.

Upstairs is the place for a fine dinner. The menu is described as Italian Fusion and some unique dishes are offered. The Italian Sashimi is a selection of marinated fresh fish, shrimp and fruit granite, calamari julienne, citronette, tuna tartare with black sauce, scallop carpaccio and vodka sour, grouper and scaramouche ceviche. The Black Ravioli has a baccala stuffing, creamed potato and pearls of black truffle.

There are wonderful lunchtime offerings too like Gorgonzola Panino salad with baby spinach, red cabbage, Gorgonzola, pears, walnuts, crispy bacon and black pepper vinaigrette. Or you could try the Shrimp and Tuna Salad with Romaine lettuce, tuna in olive oil, steamed shrimps, tomatoes, radish, cucumber, mango, orange, and a gingerette.

Breakfast is catered too – Italian coffees with breads and pastries are served with a smile.

Wherever you are and what ever time it is the Scaramouche will likely be there for you to enjoy some Italian flavor.

Specialty Drink

Orange Passion

Ingredients: Mashed Orange
                Cane Sugar
                Bitter Campari
                Orange Juice

Method: Delicately mash the orange and cane sugar.
                Mix ingredients with Italian feeling.
                Stir with love and drink with passion

Specialty Dish

Mango Tartelletta Dessert

Ingredients: 50 grms classical custard
                5 drops essence of rosewater
                200 grms sliced mango
                10 grms butter
                50 grms cane sugar
                5 drops dark rum
                Icing sugar for dusting

Method: Roll out pasta frolla and cut to fit tart molds. Prick with fork.
                Pre cook in 180 degree centigrade oven for 20 minutes.
                Allow to cool. Mix rosewater with custard.
                Melt butter and sugar in pan, add mango slices and caramelize.
                Add rum. Place the cooled custard in tart, top with caramelized
                mango and dust with icing sugar. Serve warm.
                (6 portions)

Scaramouche

Late night club atmosphere with music and dancing till late

Scaramouche

Italians know about food
They'll put you in a good mood
A handsome young man
Maybe in your plan
Is tonight the night to be wooed?

I hope they serve up gelato
But not one made with tomato
An Italian ice
Is ever so nice
Have one while strolling the parco

Cryptic Comment

When I drink I'm another man...
and he likes drinking, too
We'll always be friends because he knows too
much.

Tamarind Club

Famous for "Sunday Brunch."
Swim up Pool

Candle-lit Dinners
Delightful Rooms with AC.
Close to the Airport
Open 7 Days. Happy Hour: 4pm to 6pm

Tel: 495-2477 • Web Site www.tamarindclub.com
E-mail: tamarind@tamarindclub.com

The Tamarind Club at Josiah's Bay is a small hotel set in tropical gardens. There are nine charming rooms enveloping a fresh water pool with a swim-up bar.

The Tamarind's restaurant is famous island wide with both locals and visitors. It's open 7 days a week for breakfast, lunch and dinner and is very popular for Sunday brunch. Enjoy dishes like Eggs Benedict, Ale Battered Fish and Chips, Eric's BBQ Ribs with home-made sauce and much more.

Dinner is a quiet, candle-lit affair and the special recipe listed here, Mahi-Mahi with Coconut and Chili Sauce in a Banana Leaf is just one of many island dishes unique to the Tamarind Club. This restaurant offers theme nights such as Italian, Southern, Roast or Kebab. It's a great location for weddings, anniversaries and special events – rooms are available.

The Tamarind Club's bar 'The Centre of the Universe' is a focal point in the lounge. The attractive stone work, ambient lighting and charismatic music all add to make this spot a 'must visit.'

Reservations Please!

Liquid Sunshine

Ingredients:
- 1 shot gin
- Splash of cranberry juice
- Splash of Ting
- Squeeze of fresh lime
- Top up with bubbly

Method: Pour this delectable bubbly and sunny cocktail over ice and garnish with a lemon wedge

Specialty Dish

Baked Mahi with Coconut and Green Chili

Ingredients:
- 1/2 cup diced tomatoes
- 3 cloves roasted garlic, chopped
- 2 tbs dessicated coconut
- 1 tsp chili lime pickle
- Juice of ½ lime
- Banana leaf for wrap
- 8 oz portion of Mahi
- 1 tbs butter

Method: Sauce: Warm all sauce ingredients over low heat until well blended

Fish: Prepare banana leaf by cutting into rectangle, wipe with clean damp cloth and hold over flame until dark and soft. Sear fish over high heat. Rub banana leaf with butter and place fish on leaf and top with chili and coconut sauce. Fold into a square parcel and fasten with a toothpick or two.
Bake in 450 oven for 15 minutes

Serve with seasoned rice and fresh vegetables, extra sauce on the side.

Tamarind Club

Tamarind Club

The Tamarind Club has it all
Go there and have a ball
Try island fish
Nothing short of delish
It'll be your best port of call

The bar is right by the pool
Belly up and pull up a stool
Order your drink
There'll be glasses to clink
You won't find a bar that's more cool.

What's a man's idea of a balanced diet? A beer in each hand!

Trellis Kitchen/ Cybercafé

"The World's Best Departure Lounge"

Free Giveaway Turbokiller (2 for 1)

Fireball Full Moon Party Extravaganza
Great Breakfasts, Lunches,
   Dinners... on the Deck
Fresh Fruit Smoothies
Broadband Wireless Hotspot

Tel: 495-2447 • VHF Ch 16 • www.trelliskitchen.posthaven.com

Trellis Kitchen is one of the coolest bars and restaurants in the BVI. Located in Trellis Bay next to Aragorn's art studio it opened for business in October '01 and is now a BVI tradition. The small bar and eatery was the brainchild of Jeremy Wright, long time watersports enthusiast and windsurfing aficionado who saw a market for cyber communications and decided to incorporate it with a unique food and drinks café. Customers can sit outside in the shade overlooking the bay while enjoying unusual creations at breakfast, lunch or dinner.

There's a special island menu with bar drinks and fruit smoothies with local tropical fruits. Breakfasts can be a simple affair of muffins and coffee right through to "The Full Monty." Yep, you guessed it – a full English breakfast. Unusual items on the "24 hr meals" menu are "Croque Monsieur," an open sandwich with seven-grain bread, ham, egg and cheese. Caribbean desserts are also on the menu. There are daily specials too, Caribbean style.

The Trellis Bay full moon parties, jointly hosted by the Trellis Kitchen and Aragorn's Studio, are now the most popular party events on the island. A buffet of local Caribbean dishes is offered at a reasonable price, a reggae band, live fungi music or the sounds of a steel band can be enjoyed while dancing in the sand and unique burning fireball sculptures light up the night sky. As a climax to an incredible evening watch the antics of acrobatic mocko jumbies entertain the crowd late into the evening. This is one happening event not to be missed.

A note on the free drink: "Turbokiller." This is the BVI's famous Painkiller with extra rum and a 'floater' for that extra lift!

Specialty Drink

Dark & Stormy

Ingredients: 1 shot Gosling's Rum
              Fresh squeezed ginger root

Method: Mix together and serve over ice

Specialty Dish

Awesome Sandwich

Trellis Kitchen has a seven- grain bread specially prepared and baked by a local bakery exclusively for them. It is hand sliced and filled with one of several fresh fish of your choice or lobster or ham and melted cheese. The sandwich is completed with lettuce and tomato and a thin spread of kuchela (a green mango relish). Yumm!

Cryptic Comment

**"It may be your purpose in life
To simply serve as a warning to others"**

Trellis Kitchen/ Cybercafé

Trellis Kitchen / Cybercafé

A crazy time can be had
And the girls tend to be bad
It's not too soon
Because it's full moon
And everyone's a little bit mad

It's lunar-tic time at Trellis
The party you can embellish
Dance to the band
With your toes in the sand
Laugh with the jumbies, be devilish

The food is West Indian style
The BVI's best, by a mile
If you don't like goat water
Try it here, 'cos you ought ta
You won't see it again for a while

Cryptic Comment

**Damn right I'm good
in bed. I can stay there all day**

The Watering Hole

The Grateful Belly Garden Deli,
  Wine Shop/Bar
Central Location, Road Town.
  Al Fresco Dining
South African wines, tapas, wine tastings
  and marvelous Margarita Mondays
Open 7am to 12 midnight. Breakfast, lunch and dinner

Tel: 494-3340 • www.proudly-african.com

Free Giveaway
Zambezi Sunset
(2 for 1)

The Watering Hole is a centrally located bar and restaurant close to Village Cay Marina. Their garden setting is ideal for a cool drink and light meal. Their theme is essentially African and they have a large selection of South African wines to enjoy with your meal or takeaway. Enquire about their wine club discounts.

The Watering Hole's daytime deli is known as the Grateful Belly. Here you can have Wraps, Paninis and Salads. The choices are awesome: the Hurry Ms Curry is a wrap of chicken curry and pineapple. The fish taco comes with salsa, greens and cilantro dressing. The Eat my Fire Panini combines sweet chilli chicken, jack cheese, toasted almonds, dried cranberries, caramelized onion and parsley... Yumm! The salmon salad is made from fresh salmon, spinach, tomatoes, spring onions, baby potatoes and avocado. Hungry yet?

Don't forget that in the mornings the Watering Hole is open for coffee and breakfast... so start the day off right!

Specialty Drink

Zambezi Sunset

Ingredients:
2 shots Pineapple Rum
1 shot Limoncello
1 shot Medori (Watermelon Liqueur)
Splash of Passion Fruit Juice
Splash of Grenadine

Method:
Pour ingredients carefully over ice one at a time. Lightly swirl and finish with the splash of Grenadine. Hey Presto! A Sunset!

Specialty Dish

African Spiced Lamb Kebab

Ingredients:
Pre-cooked boneless chunks of leg of lamb
Cajun Spice
Fresh Onion Pieces
Bell Peppers, Red, Green and Yellow.
Cherry Tomatoes.
Pita Bread (in wedges)
Peach Salsa

Method:
The lamb chunks are liberally rubbed with the Cajun spice.
The ingredients are then spiked onto the skewer and grilled until done. The kebabs are served with Pita bread and peach salsa.

The Watering Hole

The Watering Hole

The Watering Hole
Has long been my goal
To go for a glass of fine wine
I've enjoyed the deli
Have a grateful belly
I chose the best place to dine

I don't give a damn
I'll be back for the lamb
It's the very best thing on their list
Then I'll drink some more wine
With some friends of mine
Pretty girls, the ones that I've missed

Cryptic Comment

**In beer there is gas,
In water there are bacteria
But in wine there is wisdom.**

Jost Van Dyke

Abe's By The Sea
Located at Little Harbour Abe's is famous for seafood dinners especially lobster. The bar is always open as long as someone's around.

Gertrude's Bar
Gertrude's is right next to the Soggy Dollar Bar in White Bay and a large selection of lounge chairs on the sand are waiting for you and your tropical cocktail.

Harris' Place
Located next to Sidney's Harris' is famous for his "all you can eat" lobster dinners on Monday nights. Ice is available here along with some groceries.

Rudy's
Rudy's is a combination, superette, bar, restaurant, and party venue at the western end of Great Harbour. Rudy sometimes plays his guitar for special parties like those that come in from the Flying Cloud, a charter "head boat." Rudy is a fisherman so fresh fish and lobster are nearly always available.

Virgin Gorda & other islands

Biras Creek
A Relais Chateau recognized restaurant. Fine food but requires dressing up. You'll need a fat wallet here.

Pancho's
Pancho's is in Gun Creek, at the end of the road. Real island style food available here and you can play pool while you're waiting.

Poor Man's Bar
Right on the beach at the famous Baths. Cold beer, drinks and sandwiches are available.

Virgin Gorda & other islands

Sugarcane
Sugarcane is the new name for the old Dog and Dolphin. Difficult to access for yachties.

Anegada Beach Club
A nice ambiance with Tiki style bar and a small pool.

Cooper Island Beach Club
Completely renovated. A great lunch stop. Can be uncomfortable in the winter months and is not recommended for overnight anchoring. If you do decide to overnight here a good meal can be had ashore.

Tortola

Big Banana
The Big Banana is right next to Rhymer's at Cane Garden Bay. They serve breakfast, lunch and dinner and prices are reasonable. There is entertainment on some nights. In the same premises are a gift shop and an ice cream stand.

Bing's Drop Inn Bar
Bing's, at East End village, is popular as a late night venue. Dancing goes on till late and bar meals can be had.

Bomba's Shack
Bomba's achieved world fame when it was featured in the Sport's Illustrated Swimsuit Edition some years back. Bomba's famous full moon parties are legendary with mushroom tea being served at midnight.

Charlie's
An up market restaurant at the Moorings. Popular with charter boat guests and local business people.

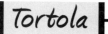
Tortola

Clem's by the Sea

Clem used to be a bartender at the pub years ago and he really knows his drinks. Not only that but he plays steel pan music so prepare to be entertained. His bar and restaurant are located in Carrot Bay across from the park. The restaurant specializes in local dishes like goat water, fish & fungi and conch.

De Wedding

Located at the western end of Cane Garden Bay: the quiet end. It has its own tyre swing.

Pub

Right on the water by Fort Burt. Access by dinghy, parking often difficult. Popular pub food available.

Pusser's

A BVI chain of restaurants and shops. Many people liken the restaurants to TGI Fridays in the US. They are well known for the islands' special drink, the Painkiller... made with Pusser's rum.

Stanley's

Some thirty-five years ago Stanley's emerged as the first beach bar in Cane Garden Bay. The restaurant became famous for lobster dinners, pina coladas and the steel pan band that played after dinner. It was the blueprint for many to follow. Outside the bar, tied to a tall overhanging palm tree, was a tire swing. Stanley's and the tire swing were featured on thousands of postcards and calendars and became the quintessential trademark of the British Virgin Islands. It's still there and many still stop by on a trip down memory lane.

... and there are still more...!

**Ali Baba's
Free BBC or Paralyser
(2 for 1)**

**Corsairs
Free Beer or Well Drink
(2 for 1)**

**Foxy's
Born 'ere Beer**

**Foxy's Taboo
Bubbly Passion
(2 for 1)**

**Ivan's Local Flavor
Rum Punch
(2 for 1)**

**One Love
Bushwacker
(2 for 1)**

**Sidney's Peace & Love
Rum Punch
(2 for 1)**

**Soggy Dollar
Painkiller**

 **Bath & Turtle's
Rendezvous Bar
Rum Punch with Lunch**

 **Bitter End Yacht Club
and Crawl Pub
Painkiller (2 for 1)**

*TOOTS
The Best*

 **Fat Virgin Café
Tropical Cocktail
(2 for 1)**

 **Jumbies Bar
at Leverick Bay
Bushwacker or Painkiller**

 **Saba Rock
Mai Tai
(2 for 1)**

 **Top of the Baths
Rum Punch
(2 for 1)**

 **Anegada Reef Hotel
Famous Rum Smoothie**

 **The Big Bamboo
Bamboo Teaser
(2 for 1)**

 **Neptune's Treasure
Bottle of Wine with
Dinner (1 per table of 4)**

 **Pirates Bite
Discounted Bushwacker**

 **Bamboushay
Any Well Drink
(2 for 1)**

 **BananaKeet Café
Bottle of Wine with
Dinner (table of 4)**

 **Brandywine Restaurant
Mojito
(2 for 1)**

**Captain Mulligan's
Round of Golf
(2 for 1)**

**CruZin
Margarita
(2 for 1)**

**D' Best Cup
2 free Coffees
with 2 Sandwiches**

**The Dove
Glass of their best
house wine with dinner**

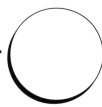

**Emile's Sports Bar & Grill
Chairman's Sweet 'n Sour
(2 for 1)**

**The Loose Mongoose
Tropial Smoothie:
'Noseeum' (2 for 1)**

**Myett's
Free Bottle of Wine
with Dinner**

**Peg Legs
Free Bottle of Wine
with Dinner**

**Quito's Gazebo
Quito's Legend
(2 for 1)**

**Rhymer's
Beach
Bar**

**Rhymer's Beach Bar
Painkiller or Rum Punch
(2 for 1)**

**Sailor's Rest
Free Bottle of Wine
with Dinner**

**Scaramouche
Orange Passion
(2 for 1)**

**Tamarind Club
Liquid Sunshine
(2 for 1)**

**Trellis Kitchen / Cybercafé
Turbokiller
(2 for 1)**

The Watering Hole
Zambezi Sunset
(2 for 1)

NOTES

NOTES

NOTES

NOTES

NOTES

NOTES

NOTES

NOTES